FIND YOUR WHISTLE

Simple Gifts Touch Hearts and Change Lives

CHRISTOPHER ULLMAN

Four-Time International Whistling Champion

Portraits by Marta Capdevila

I DEDICATE THIS BOOK TO:

My parents, Fran and Joe, who gave me the gift of whistle.

My friend Elizabeth, whose encouragement enabled all this to happen.

My wife Kristen, who demanded that I write this book.

My friend Preston, whose whistling warms my heart.

www.mascotbooks.com

FIND YOUR WHISTLE: *Simple Gifts Touch Hearts and Change Lives*

For more information, please contact:
Mascot Books
560 Herndon Parkway #120
Herndon, VA 20170
info@mascotbooks.com

Library of Congress Control Number: 2016962487

CPSIA Code: PBANG0317A
ISBN-13: 978-1-68401-020-2

Printed in the United States

WITH APPRECIATION

Thanks to these friends and family for helping to bring this book to life:

Greg Ahern, Carole Ardizzone, Naren Aryal, Susan Blaylock, Rick Bloom, Peter Brown, Marta Capdevila, Mark Cecil, Jordan DeJarnette, Elizabeth Foster, Ricky Frame, Elizabeth Gill, Jamie Gold, Stephen Gold, Ed Grenier, Larry Haas, Judy Heath, Thomas B. Heath, Thomas L. Heath, Sofia Hubscher, Jason Kelly, LoriAnn LaRocco, Sara Lee, Dave Marchick, Karin McKinnell, Margie Myers, Deepa Nanjee, Nancy Palleschi, Lindsey Poff, Matt Rees, David Rubenstein, Michael Rubin, Sarge Salman, Mark Schoenfeld, Robert Siegel, Christopher Simon, John Reed Stark, Jenna Tea, Frances Ullman, Joseph Ullman, Kristen Ullman, Susan Ullman, Tracie Van Dorpe, Avi Warga, Randall Whitestone, and Ted Wright.

Thank you for listening, encouraging, brainstorming, caring, editing, advising, suggesting, and loving.

Chris Ullman

CONTENTS

FOREWORD

By David M. Rubenstein
Co-Founder and Co-CEO, The Carlyle Group

IN 2001, an investment firm that I helped to found, The Carlyle Group, was looking to hire its first global communications director, and I had the task of finding someone to fill the position. I was not making much progress until Arthur Levitt, a former Chairman of the U.S. Securities and Exchange Commission and then a Carlyle advisor, recommend his former communications director from the SEC.

I was skeptical that a specialist in communicating about regulatory matters could actually adapt to the private sector and the investment world. But as a courtesy to Arthur, I interviewed Chris Ullman, then leading the communications activities at the George W. Bush Administration's U.S. Office of Management and Budget.

In the interview, I quickly realized how right Arthur had been—Chris was a first-rate communications professional and certainly had the experience, focus, and personality that the position required.

But Chris had another dimension to him, a unique skill that he had developed over several decades as a passionate, creative, and talented whistler. Indeed, he was a four-time international champion, who would later be inducted into the Whistling Hall of Fame.

In our interview, I thought that this skill (one I particularly admired since I could never whistle a note) was a bit of a hobby or sideline pursuit. Everyone seems to have one, after all.

However, in the fifteen years that Chris has worked at Carlyle (during which he has whistled at major Carlyle events, for Carlyle professionals' birthdays, and at numerous significant public events), I have come to realize that Chris' whistling virtuoso talent is not merely a hobby or sideline pursuit. Rather, it is an essential part of his character, as Chris explains so interestingly in this book.

Chris views his whistling ability as a vital part of his persona and as a gift he has been blessed with to give to others. And he has done so countless times over a nearly forty year period, most movingly at the birthdays, weddings, graduations, and celebrations of family, friends, acquaintances, and others needing good cheer and warm feelings, always to great appreciation and (for those who have not previously heard Chris' whistling) amazement at the musical skill that two lips puckered together can actually achieve.

Chris' book is well worth reading not just because one gets to see first-hand the pleasure Chris gets from decades of whistling for others, or even the pleasure so many others get from being on the receiving end of beautifully whistled popular and classical songs.

Rather, Chris' main point, so gracefully and humorously told, is that by having the skill to whistle in a way that creates joy in the world, he is doing what others can and should do: find their own *whistle* and use that skill or talent to bring happiness and pleasure to others. Nothing is so rewarding, in Chris' view, than for an individual to find his or her *whistle* and use it to benefit others.

In this book, Chris persuasively describes the importance—and pleasure—of finding and using one's *whistle*.

Of course, doing so may not be that easy. And Chris underplays the value of having the prerequisite of an intrinsic character gene that wants—as a life goal—to help others as an essential part of life's mission. That character gene—perhaps more than the whistling skill—is what makes Chris such an admired and respected individual.

But for all readers, whether they have that character gene—or hope they can develop it (and this book might inspire people to do so)— Chris' book is yet another pleasure that he has given to others. Indeed, this book is another form of Chris finding his *whistle*.

I am pleased and honored to know Chris, and the readers of this book will quickly realize why everyone fortunate enough to know Chris feels the same way.

And like Chris, I hope others will be inspired by his book to find their own *whistle*.

PROLOGUE

"HOW ARE YOU?"

"I'm *great*. How are you?"

"It's only 9 a.m. Why so great already?"

"Well, I'm thankful I didn't have to wrestle a four-foot shark into my raft, stab it in the eye with a screwdriver, and then eat its liver raw for breakfast this morning."

At that gory point, the elevators opened and my colleague and I exited.

"What made you think of *that*?"

"I'm reading *Unbroken* by Laura Hillenbrand, about Louis Zamperini, whose plane crashed in the Pacific during World War II. He drifted for forty-seven days before being taken captive and tortured for two years in a Japanese prisoner of war camp. Amazingly, he actually killed two small sharks and ate their livers."

"Wow."

I'd probably ruined my colleague's day.

Once again, I should have listened to my wife's good advice: "Keep your sanctimoniousness to yourself."

I love books about people who've overcome great physical and mental challenges. My all-time favorite is *Adrift*, by Steven Callahan, a first-person account of his seventy-six days at sea in an open raft. Thirty years after first reading it, I'm still paranoid about wasting water, having seen what every drop of potable water meant to him.

And there are so many more heroic tales out there. Others atop my list include Lance Armstrong and Sally Jenkins' account of Armstrong beating cancer in *It's Not About the Bike* (though I was crushed to learn that he was a doper and fraud on the bike), and the classic *Alive*, by Piers Paul Read, which tells the story of a rugby team that resorted to cannibalism after their plane crashed in the snow-bound Andes.

In each, we learn of heroic, off-the-scale, hard-to-comprehend physical endurance and mental steeliness in the face of certain death. The contrasts and juxtapositions within them are fascinating. On one hand they grip and revolt (the brutality of chemotherapy in Armstrong's book and the eating of raw bird meat and eyeballs in *Unbroken* and *Adrift*), while at the same time they encourage and motivate (showing readers that when times are tough there is a well-spring of physical and mental resolve within us).

These stories remind me to make the most of the gifts God has given me, because we never know when hardship or tragedy will strike. On a daily basis, they help me keep life in perspective and appreciate the tasty fruit smoothie and egg sandwich I have most mornings. If the greatest hardship I have today is dealing with bad traffic or a challenging person at work, then I'm doing pretty well. And those times when I face serious struggles, I'm reminded that if I dig deeper, I'll likely find untapped reserves of energy, insight, and hope.

In this spirit, *Find Your Whistle* started out as a collection of lessons learned from my nearly half-century whistling journey. But two years into the process of thinking and writing, I came to a humbling conclusion: I'm not a hero, therefore my moral authority in terms of "lessons learned" was minimal.

Yes, I've done lots of sweet, crazy, outrageous, and poignant things with my pucker, but none of them are heroic. I haven't scaled Mt. Everest blind, cured or conquered cancer, survived weeks at sea in a small raft, overcome terrific hardship or addiction, made or lost a billion dollars, or eaten raw shark liver.

I'm not a hero—just a whistler.

Back to the drawing board I went.

What do all my whistling stories, experiences, and people I've met add up to? Are they pieces to a giant coherent puzzle? Or are they random events that have nothing to do with each other?

Then, one day on a bike ride (my main form of exercise and mental therapy), the answer came to me. The fact that I *haven't* done anything heroic is the point. That I've taken a simple, common ability—whistling—and used it to touch people's hearts and lives in simple and unexpected ways (and, in doing so, have had an awesome, kick-butt, thoroughly entertaining and enlightening time) is the point.

Those hearts belong to all sorts of people: male, female, rich, poor, young, old, happy, sad, powerful, weak, friend, stranger, black, white, straight, gay, able-bodied, developmentally challenged, American, foreigner, you name it.

As I surveyed my nearly fifty years of whistling, I concluded that my simple gift is a key that gives me access to people's hearts. Like a skeleton key that can open any lock, my whistle can penetrate most any heart—because no matter who someone is or their station in life, we are all part of a giant family, and our common bond is our humanity. And, by definition, every human has a heart, however much my children sometimes question whether I have one. (I'm not a big pet person, which, according to my three kids, means I must be missing a heart.)

Far along this new path, I started to wonder if the simple and heroic still might be connected in some way. Might they be opposite sides of the same coin, or counterbalancing weights on a barbell? Near and far bookends on a shelf, or peanut butter and jelly?

Pick your visual. Select a metaphor. The point, I've come to believe, is that the heroic and the simple are both necessary in life, to inspire us on one hand and give us daily purpose and local impact on the other.

There is much to be learned from the blind mountain climber, the person who beats cancer, the war hero. How did they prepare their minds and bodies for the challenge? Where did they find energy and resolve when all seemed lost? Why did they not give up when all reasonable hope was long gone? How did seemingly normal people do superhuman things?

Having read lots of these books, the answers to these rather existential questions are embedded in my brain and heart and have helped me overcome all sorts of challenges. And for that I am grateful.

At the same time, though, as their experiences and achievements flirt with the superhuman, it becomes harder and harder for regular humans to relate to their successes on a daily basis.

For most of us, day-in and day-out life is all about routine, working through the checklist: eating, commuting, studying, cleaning, working, tending to children, trying to relax or exercise. If you're a parent, success may be as simple as a well-fed kid nestled safely in bed after homework is done.

In the midst of the routine and ordinary—that is where the simple thrives. The concept of *Finding Your Whistle* is so powerful because it puts aside the quest for or reliance on heroic achievement, and gives license to us mere mortals to find and develop our simple gifts, our *whistles*, and then share them with the people in our lives, friend and stranger alike.

If you're the president of the United States, your gift (your *whistle*) impacts a nation or the heart of a parent of a fallen soldier. If you're a rock star like Billy Joel or Mick Jagger, your *whistle* brings joy to jam-packed stadiums. If you're a teacher, your *whistle* touches a class or a student in need of a boost. If you're a doorman in New York City, then your *whistle* welcomes home a tired tenant at the end of the day.

And if you become known for your actual whistling skills, as I have, then your *whistle*, literal and figurative, can lead you to do things you never could have imagined: touch the hearts of presidents and Wall Street bankers, honor America through "The Star Spangled Banner" at major league sporting events, celebrate the lives of special needs children, lead 60,000 people at the U.S. Capitol in a mass whistle-in, and serenade 400 people on their birthdays every year.

And whether you're a president, a star performer, or a PR guy, your *whistle* has to come from somewhere. Mine started on a day like any other. In the town of Massapequa Park, on the south shore of New York's Long Island, in the backyard of a house on Lake Shore Drive, at the foot of my father when I was only five years old, I discovered a great gift. I found my whistle.

That moment, when air and lips and tongue conspired to form a sound unlike any my little body had ever produced, was memorable. The sound was anemic and out of tune; it startled me, but delighted my father. It may not have rivaled my first step, but it was the first step on my whistling journey.

It's a journey that went from peripheral to my life to the core of my existence. It's a journey I never could have imagined, and one that continues to boggle my mind, even after all these years. Whistling has changed my life. It has exposed me to bizarre, heartening, and awkward situations, and introduced me to all sorts of people. It has tested my confidence and made me rise to occasions that would have otherwise terrified me into inaction.

But most importantly, whistling has allowed me to enter people's hearts and lives in ways that have humbled and inspired me, and given me deep satisfaction and joy.

That's what has kept me going through the years, especially after I stopped competing in the international whistling competition in 2004. Sharing my whistle has given deeper purpose to my gift…and my life. Yes, I still whistle in the car, while walking down the street, and in the parking garage and stairwells at work (great acoustics), because I truly enjoy bringing great music to life, rather than just thinking about it. But knowing that I can make people happy with my whistle is really what motivates me.

Ask anyone who volunteers in the community or gives back in some way, and they will invariably say they get more from the experience than they gave, whether it's joy or humility or the satisfaction of having made a difference. This is one of the especially fascinating things about humans. We do good things for people, often strangers, expecting nothing tangible in return. The feeling of being relevant, of mattering, of feeling that your presence made a difference, is a powerful intangible reward.

In 1984, I did a crazy thing. I circumnavigated the U.S. alone on a motorcycle. Along the nearly 9,000-mile journey, I waved and gave the peace sign to many people in their cars and eighteen-wheelers as we zoomed by each other. I was twenty-one years old and generally scared and lonely, and it was a way to connect with other living creatures. When people responded, it made me feel good and it validated my existence, especially on desolate roads in the middle of nowhere.

I think that's at the core of why I whistle "Happy Birthday" to so many people.

To me, life is the most precious gift we have, so acknowledging it is important, and birthdays are the perfect excuse. Sending a card or calling people on their birthdays is a wonderful way to show those people that they matter, that their presence on this earth is a good thing, that you are glad they were born.

While I don't whistle for people to elicit thanks, having someone say "You made my day," after receiving a birthday serenade is so special. I hear it a lot, and try hard to always appreciate what it actually means. "You made my day" is like that person saying "Thank you for caring…for making me feel special."

And it makes me happy too. It makes me feel relevant, like I matter too, like my whistle is doing good in the world.

Yes, I've found my *whistle*.

So, dear reader, how about you? Have you found your *whistle*?

Finding your *whistle* may be as simple as putting name to something you may already be doing. Whether your *whistle* is hiding in plain sight or yet to be discovered, the key is to be volitional about it—to find, develop, and share your *whistle*. And it's easier to develop and share a talent or skill if you have given name to it.

One time, I gave a talk to the board of directors of the Junior Achievement of Greater Washington. JA, as it's known, teaches children around the world about financial literacy, work readiness, and entrepreneurship. It's a great organization whose purpose is in greater need than ever.

After the event, where I talked about finding one's *whistle*, a young man in his early-thirties approached me and we started chatting. Soon enough, he admitted that he didn't know what his *whistle* was. I asked him a bunch of questions to get a better sense of who he was and what was important to him.

He was an African-American man who grew up in the inner city, went to college, got a job at a major U.S. bank, and was passionate about helping people in lower income areas get access to banking services (especially loans) to build small businesses and create jobs. I was mesmerized by this young man. His passion was contagious, especially as he spoke of an experience he had had years before that set him on a path to want to give back to his community.

"You've already found your *whistle*," I exclaimed.

He was instantly curious, in a somewhat suspicious way, about my claim.

"You could give a TEDx talk on your journey," I practically pleaded with him.

The more we talked, the clearer it became to him that he had a *whistle*. The blending of his passion and skill with his day job touched the lives of many and gave him joy, but he hadn't given it a name. But a *whistle* by any other name is still a *whistle*.

As we said goodbye, I could see the gears turning in his brain as he thought about the implications of being more volitional with his gift. Might he be able to touch more lives? Inspire more people to follow in his footsteps? Help change the face of a community, giving financial might to people's dreams? Yes, yes, and more yes.

I loved chatting with this man. His passion and enthusiasm inspired me. It's encouraging to meet someone fired up for a cause. That's how I knew in an instant that he had found his *whistle*. He has fashioned his smarts and passion and his bank's balance sheet into a simple gift that was making a difference in the lives of people in our community. Now, that's a good reason to whistle a happy tune.

And I've had many similar conversations with people through the years. It's powerful and exciting to discover or reveal a *whistle* that's been there all along. Think of Dorothy's revelation at the end of *The Wizard of Oz*: "There's no place like home; there's no place like home." Safely home in Kansas after her reality-bending journey, Dorothy realizes that she didn't need to leave her home and family to live the life she wanted; the people and ingredients were already there, waiting to be discovered.

I've met many people in recent years who swear they don't have a *whistle*. It's a combination of humility and fear, I believe, that keeps people from thinking they have a gift that can make a difference. They seem hung up on the hero model, thinking that only heroes have something to teach and that only heroes can solve problems, especially big ones.

This could not be more false. Despite my love of books about triumph over adversity, those remarkable people are not able to solve all the world's problems. They couldn't if they tried. There are just too many. The only way to truly make the world a happier, safer, healthier, and more joyous place is to harness the energy and talents and passions—the *whistles*—of countless everyday people who want to make a difference, to touch hearts and change lives.

To those sceptics, I say everyone has a *whistle*, large or small, fancy or plain. There's something simple in each of us that can make the world a better place. I bring up the concept of having a *whistle* in all sorts of circumstances—at kids' soccer games, business meetings, cocktail parties, and meals with friends with strangers alike. I have to be careful to not come across as self-righteous, the guy with all the answers to life's deep questions. It's always been my nature to want to get to know people and talk about things other than the weather, so conversations can readily stray into "meaning of life" type topics. My approach is to share what works for me and see what works for them, then hopefully we all walk away smarter and energized about how to make the most of every day.

As I look at the development of my own whistle, time has been a great friend. Like a mustard seed, my *whistle* started out small and anemic, and has grown to be lush and fruitful. As you'll see throughout this book, I worked hard to develop it. Hopefully you'll get a kick out of Chapter 23, which details a crazy Graceland pilgrimage I did before the 1996 international competition. I whistled five hours a day for a week while circumnavigating the state of Tennessee in my convertible red Miata. Yes, I was alone...even I could hardly stand *that* much whistling!

So, I didn't start out trying to change the world...and I haven't. I have worked to make my little corner of it a little brighter. I'm part of a giant mosaic, as are you and lots of other people, whose individual actions come together, like tiny colored stones, to form a picture and tell a story of boundless ingenuity, initiative, talent, and love.

While *Find Your Whistle* is about how I found, developed, and have shared my whistle with friends and strangers, to help illustrate the range of *whistles* out there, you'll soon meet ten people whose metaphorical *whistles* have touched my heart and life in some special way. These people—John A., Kelly, Tony, John H., Rocky, Tom, Michael, John S., Fran and Dan—have found their *whistles*, developed them, and are sharing them. They have embraced their roles as part of the great mosaic of life.

People often ask why I like to whistle. To some extent, I whistle because I whistle; there's a certain amount of inertia to it. It's been such a part of my life for so long—nearly fifty years—that it's as much a part of me as my pale Irish skin and kinky hair. But driving the momentum of those five decades of puckering and blowing is the joy that comes from making music happen, whether I'm entertaining myself on the drive into work or brightening someone's day with a "Happy Birthday" serenade.

My whistle, an unwitting gift from my parents, has changed the course of my life. I am so blessed to have figured out that it could be an instrument, literally and figuratively, for good in the world.

So, as you delve into the journey of how I found *my whistle* and have used this simple gift to touch hearts and change lives, I hope these stories will tickle your fancy as you find *your whistle*.

CHAPTER 1
Beethoven and Banjos in the Oval Office

THE SENIOR STAFF gathered outside Mitch Daniels' office. It was 8:25 in the morning on June 20, 2001. We were in the OEOB, Washington-speak for the Old Executive Office Building, a spectacular example of French Second Empire architecture, only 125 feet or so from the West Wing of the White House.

I stood beside a TV resting on a waist-high table next to the massive oak door that separated the large and brightly lit reception area from the black and white checkerboard marble floor hallway. It was the same TV that less than three months later would break the news to the nation's top budget official that terrorists had just crashed planes into the Twin Towers of the World Trade Center.

The first day of summer was sunny and warm. George W. Bush was five months into his presidency. The budgeteers at the U.S. Office of Management and Budget (OMB) were working long hours, turning Bush's campaign promises to cut taxes and slow government spending into reality, to the delight of some and the chagrin of others.

Surrounded by top experts in every aspect of federal programs, my job as head of communications was to turn these green-eye shade topics into plain English, so everyday Americans could better understand what the federal government was doing with their hard-earned money...more than $2 trillion annually in those days. Today, only fifteen years later, that number is $3.8 trillion.

The director's door opened with a rush, and flock-like, the twelve senior staff instinctively moved toward the void. Unexpectedly, Mitch, the federal government's top budget guru, said the meeting was cancelled, but that I should stay. I got a few *good luck* looks from colleagues as they went back to the grindstone. I quickly looked at Mitch's face to get a better sense of his mood, but he was already on his way back into his spacious, ornate office.

As a professional spokesman, I've long said that I'm one bad quote away from losing my job. Telling the world about the new president's first budget, which sought to cut lots of programs, was a high wire act. Maybe I had annoyed someone in the West Wing—perhaps even the president himself.

From the moment we issued the budget in mid-February 2001 (which was a few days before I got married), the budgeteers at OMB were under attack. Beach renourishment was my favorite example. The budget proposed having beachfront communities pay more to repair shores that had lost sand from storms and erosion. You'd have thought we asked people to hand over their firstborn children. It was only sand, but with 12,383 miles of coastline, we should have been better prepared for the onslaught.

Nonetheless, day after day, I was effectively the only administration official defending the cuts. Not before or since have I been quoted in so many seaside newspapers, telling citizens they needed to pay more because people in the heartland shouldn't have to pay for their new sand. Senators, representatives, state legislators, city councils, and town managers all complained bitterly. We got our hats handed to us, and after a few months of beatings, we dropped the proposal. Who knows how many senators I enraged by stressing fiscal prudence and tax fairness, when what mattered most was getting re-elected?

I took a step toward Mitch's office, glancing left at his assistant

Karen, hoping for a hint of what awaited me. Karen displayed no emotion in response to my silent inquiry. Musing for a moment, I wondered how the president felt about beaches, especially since his family had a famous beachside estate in Kennebunkport, Maine. Into the director's office I walked.

Mitchell E. Daniels, Jr. is short, bald, and wiry. After you shake his hand, he recoils a little so as not to get too close—an unusual trait for a politician; nonetheless, he later went on to win two elections as governor of Indiana.

What Mitch lacks in height and girth, he makes up in intelligence and wit. When we released the president's first budget in February of 2001, he and I conspired to do it a little differently than in previous years. Wanting to remind the public that budgeting is about making tough decisions, I gave cassette tapes (yes, they were still available in 2001) of the Rolling Stones classic "You Can't Always Get What You Want" to several reporters along with the new budget. Reporters were surprised and amused. Several of the ensuing stories referenced the unusual addition to the budget, a humorous plea for fiscal prudence.

The White House, however, was not amused, and pulled the plug on our efforts before I finished giving out the tapes to the whole White House press corps. I guess W wasn't a fan of the Stones.

Mitch loved it. The White House got over it. Yes, it is easier to seek forgiveness than ask permission...if you're a member of the president's Cabinet. That little act helped establish Mitch as a plain-English straight-shooter, which proved to be more beneficial than his budget-cutting zeal was detrimental.

Mitch's office was a grand space on the second floor of the OEOB, with tall ceilings, maybe twenty feet high, and a balcony overlooking Pennsylvania Avenue. Mitch was standing next to his desk, which was beside a large conference table. He sported a Cheshire grin, which relaxed me a bit.

"We're going to the Oval Office to whistle for the president," he deadpanned in his staccato Midwestern twang.

"Huh? Now?"

"Yes. Now. Get your jacket and let's go."

My concern over being summoned into the director's office was instantly replaced with manic excitement. A ton of questions flooded my brain: *How did this happen? Was I properly dressed? What would I whistle? Did I have time to warm-up? Could I bring my wife?*

As I walk-ran to my office one floor up, the puzzle pieces started to come together.

Around a month before, I had encountered a friend on the sidewalk outside the OEOB. She asked if I could come to Andy Card's surprise party the next day and whistle "Happy Birthday." It's not every day you get invited to serenade the president's chief of staff in the West Wing of the White House, but I couldn't resist kidding around, gazing at my watch, silently wondering if I could make the time. A moment later, I had excitedly said I'd be honored to join them.

Though I worked in the Executive Office of the President as the budget spokesman, I didn't know a lot of the folks in the West Wing, primarily because I hadn't worked on the campaign to get Bush elected. During the 2000 election, I had worked in the Clinton administration as the spokesman for the U.S. Securities and Exchange Commission, the stock market regulator. When I had taken that job in 1997, many people had said I'd never again work for a Republican as a political appointee, that I was a traitor. So, it was with relief and the welcome realization that the conventional wisdom wasn't always right that I got an even more senior job in the Bush administration.

At the appointed early-afternoon hour, I had walked over to a conference room next to Andy Card's office in the West Wing. Unlike OEOB, West Wing offices are mostly modest in size. In the West Wing, proximity to the Oval Office trumps the size of one's office. Heck, a closet down the hall from the president beats a cavernous office across the street any day.

Mingling, chatting, and sipping were a mix of the famous (the senior administration officials who regularly appeared on cable TV) and the worker-bees (those who burned the midnight oil). A few feet away stood Condoleezza Rice, national security advisor and future secretary of state. Moments after I had quietly slipped in, Karl Rove arrived with fanfare. Karl, the architect of the Bush ascendancy to the White House, though a man of modest proportions, is quite a large presence. He lets you know he's arrived with his booming voice and ready laugh. And there was Alberto Gonzales, the top White House lawyer and future U.S. attorney general, as well as Harriet Miers, the White House staff secretary, whose future nomination to the Supreme Court crashed moments after it was launched.

And then the birthday boy arrived, properly surprised (or so he indicated). Within moments, I went from obscurity—most people had no idea who I was, or that I was even there—to the center of attention. The friend who had invited me introduced me as the four-time international whistling champion (and OMB spokesman) who was going to serenade the chief of staff.

I took a final sip of ice water, assumed the position (left foot slightly ahead, left hand raised above my waist, right hand by my side, leaning slightly forward), surveyed the room, and as my eyes landed on the guest of honor, out came the first notes. I always do a brief dramatic introduction before starting the official "Happy Birthday" tune, the same way flourishes announce the arrival of a king or dignitary. It was over in a flash—forty-one seconds, to be exact.

The assembled White House bigwigs and worker bees clapped, Andy shook my hand, and soon after I was walking back to the OEOB, alone in my thoughts, with a happy tune on my lips. I had just whistled for a man who worked 100 hours a week organizing the life of the leader of the free world.

A few days later, Mitch had told me that the president had asked about me, Andy having told him of the serenade. That was startling. Didn't the president have other things to worry about?

Yes, but presidents are people too.

I've worked for fantastically successful businesspeople for many years now. They own jets, have billions of dollars, socialize with heads of state, and make headlines with their business deals and outsized philanthropy.

Sure, they are smart, incredibly hardworking, and blessed with good timing and judgment, but they are human just like the rest of us, with the same arrays of angst, moral failings, and, in Bush's case, curiosities.

Our society's cult of personality idolizes and idealizes people, stripping them of the complexity that defines every person. So, between speaking with heads of state and investing billions of dollars, the powerful and rich sometimes pause to find wonder in simple things—even whistling.

Thinking about this previous experience whistling in the White House, I grabbed my sport coat—*darn! Should have worn a suit.* Like the motherly admonition to always wear clean underwear in case you have to go the hospital, it's best to wear a suit to work in case you get summoned to the Oval Office. I'd keep that in mind for future reference.

Despite the rush, I squeezed in one phone call to my wife from my desk.

"No, you can't come!" I sadly and hurriedly informed her.

I ran back to Mitch's office, where he was at the door, ready to go.

As we walked down the grand stone staircase, I started to warm up, a few random notes at first, and then a tune, "In the Mood," by Glenn Miller. That captured the moment, a once-in-a-lifetime chance to perform privately for the president of the United States in the Oval Office. The acoustics in stairwells are good in general, but OEOB's are like a concert hall, with five stories of sweeping stone resonance. Back in 1888, when OEOB was completed, fire codes were primitive at best, and stairwells were built to be functional *and* beautiful, not just utilitarian like they are today.

In between bursts of practice notes, Mitch and I hatched a mischievous plan. We'd do a duet: "Dueling Banjos," from the classic 1972 film *Deliverance*, but we'd do it with a twist. Mitch, who also likes to whistle, is what I call a ventrilo-whistler; like a ventriloquist, his lips don't move, and the notes seem to be coming from somewhere else. So, we'd duel in the Oval Office, but the president wouldn't know where the second sound was coming from.

Fool the president? As the first President George H.W. Bush might have said, *doesn't seem prudent.*

Mitch was adamant. Not to worry, he said, we'd be fine. Easy for him to say; it would be harder to fire a member of the Cabinet than a spokesman—especially one who didn't seem to like sand. Meanwhile, once Mitch and I resolved how our banjos would duel, I fretted over what else I should whistle.

"Don't you have some standards ready to go?" Mitch asked.

"Sure, I'm going through them now."

In the previous five months, my duties had taken me to the West Wing a few dozen times. The West Wing of the White House is like a morgue...quiet, reverential, people move deliberately...a deadly serious place. It's nothing like the old TV show *The West Wing*, which made the place look like the trading floor of the New York Stock Exchange.

At key entrances, doorways, and intersections, Secret Service agents, in dark suits with unseen but easily accessible firepower, protect the president. Eyes alone move as you pass by, assessing your motives, even if you have a White House pass hanging from your neck.

There's a point beyond which lies the entrance to the Oval Office. My previous West Wing jaunts had never taken me down that path, although Mitch had traversed it scores of times. Traveling with him allowed me free passage. Our pace slowed as we greeted the president's assistant seated outside the curved door to the Oval (as insiders called it). Our conversation ceased. We were told the president was ready to see us.

Mitch walked in first and I a step behind. At that moment, I caught my first close-up view of George W. Bush, the forty-third president of the United States of America, leaning back in his chair, feet on his desk, unlit cigar in his hand. Only then did I fully realize how freaky this whole thing was. I could hardly believe it was happening. I was on a conveyor belt...the president had ordered a serenade, and I was about to deliver it. I wasn't nervous, which was good, because I can choke if I get too nervous (more on that later). I was giddy...in awe. This was amazing. Unbelievable, actually.

I had seen the Oval Office before on a tour of the West Wing, but had never been inside. It's a rather comfy place, smaller than you'd think. It really is oval, hence the curved door. Warm hues of yellow and beige prevail. The presidential seal—a fierce bald eagle clutching arrows and olive branches—dominated the carpet I was standing on.

At his first glimpse of Mitch and me, the president dislodged his feet from his desk, jumped up, and moved swiftly to greet us.

"Do you need some water? Do you want to sit or stand?" the president asked as he shook my hand. "What do whistlers need?"

"Mr. President, nice to meet you. I'm fine, ready to go."

"How'd you learn to whistle?"

"My father taught me when I was five years old."

Without hesitation, he moved back to his desk, took out a notecard and said, "I'm going to write a review for your father when we're done."

He sat down, put his feet back on the desk, leaned back, and asked me to whistle a few tunes for him. "Country-western," was his response to my question about what type of music he liked.

Uh-oh.

I don't know much country music. I should have heeded the old lawyerly admonition of not asking a question you don't know the answer to.

But a miracle occurred, and a song popped into my head, and out came the name. "How about *The Lone Ranger* song?"

"Perfect!" The president was excited.

I didn't have the heart to tell him that the theme song to the classic 1930s radio series *The Lone Ranger* was actually the finale of the *William Tell Overture*, an Italian opera by Gioachino Rossini. But then, maybe he thought *I* was confused.

The Lone Ranger song has been in my repertoire since my childhood. I learned it from an amazing album called *120 Music Masterpieces*, which my parents bought when I was still single digits old.

At first I wasn't sure how to approach this situation. Was it a *meeting* or a *gig*? Something clicked in my brain—maybe it was the president's obvious good mood—and I went into performance mode, which is all about having fun entertaining the audience, regardless of who or how many. Whether it's a one-on-one "Happy Birthday" whistle for a friend, teaching a class of twenty third graders, doing the national anthem before 20,000 at an NBA game, or serenading the president of the United States, fun happens when I do my best and the audience is exposed to the beauty of what high-level whistling can be.

I launched into a spirited *Lone Ranger*, skipping repeated passages, not knowing how much my audience of one wanted to hear or how much time was allotted for this impromptu concert. Not long into that first piece, I mentally pinched myself, thinking, *Dude, this is the freakiest think you have ever done…it's never going to happen again…so you'd better make the most of it.*

As the last notes were absorbed into Oval Office history, the president clapped and smiled. I smiled, filled with relief. Mitch smiled, realizing I wasn't going to embarrass him. Whether you're a whistler or not, it's important to never make the boss look bad in front of his boss, especially when the big boss is *the* president.

"Now do something hard!"

"That was hard," I instinctively retorted.

Perhaps a little jazz and some improvisation would impress him. I cranked out a tasty version of Duke Ellington and Billy Strayhorn's "Take the 'A' Train," which brought a cheer from the Commander in Chief.

I then asked if he liked classical music. Without hesitation, he said, "Not Bach," but added, "Why don't you ask the vice president what he'd like to hear?" While I had been merrily riffing away, Mr. Cheney, Andy Card, Albert Gonzales, and a few other members of the White House staff had joined us. With my back to the door and absorbed by my tuneful meandering, I hadn't noticed their arrival.

With a nod of greetings, I asked the Veep, "How about some Beethoven?"

"That sounds good," he said, so I did a CliffsNotes version of the first movement of the Fifth Symphony.

Cheers all around.

The already surreal experience had grown quite beyond anything I had ever expected. Here I was, whistling and chatting with the leaders of the free world in the inner sanctum of the people's house.

Again, I reminded myself that I'd better make the most of it, absorb each detail, and enjoy every moment, as this was a once-in-a-lifetime experience. Good thing there was a photographer there…without evidence, no one would believe it happened. (Several months later, the day I left my job at OMB and returned to the private sector, a package of photos of the encounter bid me a fond farewell. Proof, thank God! One of the photos was even autographed by the president.)

The president asked for more. I respectfully said, "I don't want to over-do it."

"Don't worry," he said, "I'll let you know when I've had enough!"

That was surely the most memorable line of the visit. Just then, Director Daniels started whistling the opening call of "Dueling Banjos."

Our prank worked perfectly. The audience heard the sound and assumed it was coming from me, but I was clearly not whistling. I looked around in faux confusion, but responded on cue to Mitch's call, which elicited another volley of notes. Within a few moments, everyone figured out what was going on. With Mitch's cover blown, we were able to make it clear we were dueling with each other. Considering we hadn't rehearsed the whole song, it went rather well. Hoots and applause greeted the end of the battle. Everyone enjoyed it.

Oddly, in the middle of the concert, someone's made a random comment about the defense budget. I said we were working hard to explain it to the public. With an edge of seriousness, the president said we needed to do a better job.

"Yes, sir," seemed like the only acceptable response under the circumstances.

Then the president pivoted back to the joy of the moment, asking for a final tune that would "get us going for the day."

Inspired by the august setting, a song I love but had never whistled in public came to mind.

As the first notes of "The Battle Hymn of the Republic" left my lips, I felt like a skier who had just plunged down a double black diamond trail in a back bowl at Vail in Colorado. It was a controlled fall—exhilarating, terrifying. I was confident in my own abilities, but unsure of what was ahead.

I started off with a slow tempo and staccato style, emphasizing each note to heighten the drama. *Mine eyes...have seen...the glo—ry of... the co—ming of...the Lord.* Then I picked up the pace and shifted to a gospel and blues style for the "Glory, Glory, Hallelujah" chorus before slowing it down at the end.

My mind was singing the words as my lips produced the notes: "In the beauty of the lilies, Christ was born across the sea, with a glory in His bosom that transfigures you and me; as He died to make men holy, let us die to make men free, while God is marching on."

I was in the zone. I was consumed with making music, shaping the sound, telling a story with notes. Though still the focal point, my audience receded into the distance. I was rushing toward them with my music. I had launched off a giant mogul and was flying through the air.

And then it was over. The final notes were absorbed into history. I had landed safely. I suppressed an urge to let out a loud whoop as the clapping and cheers filled the Oval Office.

In a final gracious act, the president turned to the notecard on his desk and wrote: "Bub, Chris came by the Oval to share his magic. Best regards. Your friend, George Bush."

The president put the note in an envelope, addressed it, licked it, sealed it and asked that I hand-deliver it.

What a joy it was to present this handwritten whistling "review" to my father. The note now sits on his mantle in a clear Lucite frame.

Before we departed the Oval, the president said he was auditioning me for a state dinner. Those are the fancy wingdings presidents throw for visiting heads of state. Bush was not much of a presidential partyer (unlike his predecessor Bill Clinton), so in his eight years in office, he had only six of the grand affairs.

No invitation ever came. One concert for one head of state would have to suffice.

As Mitch and I departed, so did the other visitors. Mitch caught up with Andy Card, which left me walking beside and chatting amiably and inconsequentially with Dick Cheney. It then struck me that they had all come for the concert. I had presumed that they were just in the Oval Office for a previously scheduled meeting, and Mitch and I had been the interlopers.

Like love, music is a universal language. And whistling, perhaps second only to the human voice, is the oldest natural instrument. There are lots of reasons whistling is considered more novelty than art, but for nearly fifty years, I've marveled at how this puckered pursuit transcends age, politics, culture, gender, wealth—you name it.

When a president interrupts his busy schedule for a whistling respite, you know that there is universal appeal. Perhaps it's the wonder and sweetness in whistling. Or its simplicity that attracts while its complexity marvels. Possibly it's just the freakiness quotient, like the appeal of the suffering souls of yesteryear's carnival sideshows. Whatever the reason, whistling is a throwback to a time before gadgets entertained us, when innocence was virtuous.

Before my philosophic musings got the best of me, Mitch the budget geek was back, and reality was reinstated: "Nicely done," he intoned. "Back to work."

CHAPTER 2
Pucker Up and Blow: The Championship Path

"YOU *WRESTLE?*" he asked over the din of the live music in the bar.

"No, whistle! Like this…" Puckering up, I let out a few notes and watched his brow furrow a bit.

"Oh. I'll see what I can do."

At least I'm on the list, I thought as I made my way to a seat at the back of the Sunset Grille, a casual burger and wings joint in Annandale, Northern Virginia that doubled as a blues club at night. Whether I'd ever get summoned to the front to jam with the band was another story.

The first time I'd whistled with a band was in college. I was at a small bar in Binghamton, New York, listening to a friend's jazz band play. Out of the blue, a thought had popped in my head: *wouldn't it be fun to jam with the band?*

At the break, I'd asked my buddy, a laid-back saxophone-player, if he'd be open to me sitting in with them on a tune. Eric was aware of my whistling, and without hesitation, said yes.

"What song do you want to do?"

Like the proverbial dog who'd finally caught the car, I hadn't thought that far ahead.

"Hhhmmm?" I thought out loud.

"How about a basic upbeat blues tune?" he suggested.

"Okay, that works. When do I come in?"

"We'll do the head, then I'll jam a bit, then throw it to you."

"Cool," I said. *Aaaahhhh! What's a head? And what if I dropped his throw?*

Two songs into the next set, I got the nod from Eric to come on stage. As he handed me a microphone, he told the audience of twenty or so that I was a whistler. I heard a "Yeah, man," emanate from the dark, and a few people clapped. Someone giggled.

Eric nodded his head three times, and his band came alive with sound. I glanced at each of them and was comforted by their smiles and looks of *I've never seen this before but, hey, I'm cool with it.* That eased my nervousness.

The notes flowed from each instrument, the parts becoming a whole. Even though I hadn't whistled a note, I felt different. I was no longer a passive observer. I was now in the band producing the music. I was a cog in the machine, and my shot at turning the musical crank was rapidly approaching.

Eric's eyes were closed. His cheeks puffed and deflated as he breathed life into his tenor saxophone. An accomplished jazz musician, Eric handled his instrument with the confidence of a Formula One driver on a twisty track. Since this was a blues jam, there was no discernible tune, but the rhythm and tempo were clear and a general feeling quickly emerged. As his riff came to an end, a silly thought popped in my head: *what was I going to whistle?*

But then his eyes opened and locked on mine.

And with a nod, it was my turn. I caught his pass and started running.

Notes came out. I don't know which ones or why, but I appeared to be in the right key. I grabbed the theme, I think, and twisted and toyed with it. Eyes closed, I tried to stay in sync with the bass and drums as they kept a crisp rhythm. That same guy let out another "Yeah, man." A few people clapped.

But I wasn't sure when to stop.

Then the rhythm guitarist shifted to lead and merged alongside me.

That must be my cue. I hit the exit ramp and lowered the microphone. The place erupted with hoots and applause. The freak show was over, but people had enjoyed it. Eric gave me a big smile.

I started whistling at five years old. My father, Joseph "Bub" Ullman, an avid whistler, paved the way with his own incessant music-making around the house and yard in Massapequa Park on Long Island, New York. Throughout my youth, especially on weekends, whether we were doing chores or tossing the Frisbee, Pop and I could be found whistling a happy tune.

His songs of choice were Gilbert and Sullivan. Mine were classical and romantic: Beethoven, Strauss (Richard and Johann), Tchaikovsky, Mozart, and Rachmaninoff.

To this day, my eighty-two year-old father has distinct recollections of me following him around the house and yard, helping and whistling. Those earliest days are especially hazy for me; I don't know if I actually remember, or if Pop's stories and photos from that period are doing the remembering for me.

Classical symphonic music dominated my entire pre-teen life. It wasn't until fourteen or so that I branched out into rock, pop, show tunes, and later blues and jazz.

In those early years, my parents had a small collection of vinyl albums and a record player nestled in a honking piece of furniture in the living room. Inside a nook in the coffee table in the middle of the room was a stack of albums. My favorites were the Johann Strauss, Jr. waltzes and a collection of the world's finest classical music called *120 Music Masterpieces*. These albums featured snippets of famous classical tunes. It was a musical buffet, a smorgasbord of the greatest composers, symphony orchestras, and soloists.

Anyone who grew up in the New York metropolitan area in the 1970s likely remembers the TV commercials with John Williams, a crusty old British actor, singing the praises of the 120 snippets, noting that even the "Polovetsian Dance #2" by Borodin was included. My mom mail-ordered those albums, and I played them incessantly. This multi-album set plus two albums of Johann Strauss Jr. waltzes provided fodder for years of whistling practice. Forty-five years later, if I hear one of the 120 snippets, I joyously whistle along and even know what song comes next, the tunes and song order indelibly etched in my brain.

It was a great blessing that my parents and siblings never harassed me about my whistling. They either actually liked it or (more likely) learned to tolerate it. As I've heard over the years, many people don't like whistling. The sound can be too high-pitched and piercing. As an infant, our son Justus hated whistling. Any time I whistled while holding him, he'd push my face away and say, "No sing, Daddy. No sing."

Easily the most formative period in my whistling development was my early teen years. From thirteen to sixteen, I whistled two hours a day while delivering newspapers. I'd get home from school, mount my Schwinn Stingray, pick up the papers a half-mile from our house, and take care of my fifty or so customers.

Whistling was my friend, but it also filled a void. I have always liked to be busy. Deep inside of me, there is a passion for movement, for productivity. So, though my legs were busy pedaling, my brain wasn't doing much. A missed opportunity! Looking back, whistling while delivering papers was my first real attempt at multi-tasking. Spinning legs and puckered lips—it sounds like a scene from *The Wonder Years* TV show.

In those paper delivery days, it was more about volume than quality. My customers often said, "I heard you coming." But over time, mush turned to marvel. One time in college, I was walking out of a grocery store whistling. A man coming toward me in the parking lot recognized the tune and said, "Beethoven. Second piano concerto." That was encouraging. I was able to hear Beethoven in my head and make it come out my lips. And he even seemed to enjoy it…bonus. Perhaps that's how actors feel when they are recognized on the street for the first time.

I dabbled in musical instruments in my youth…recorder, drums, clarinet...not achieving much proficiency in any of them. Singing in choirs, though, was the constant that made me a musician. Through high school and for twelve years post-college, I sang in two choirs. Larry Holdridge and Betty Buchanan, my high school and Washington, DC conductors, respectively, were central to my musical formation. They brought notes to life, infusing them with joy and passion. They were wonderful teachers, explaining and motivating and shaping.

Betty, especially, taught me true musicianship, how to turn notes into music. In those dozen years, she never raised her voice, even when us choristers had obviously not practiced enough on our own or were goofing off. She was patient and determined and gentle and joyous and loving.

Through Betty, I learned how to combine technical mastery and interpretive ability. Playwright Tom Stoppard well captured the elusiveness of this goal when he said, "Skill without imagination is craftsmanship and gives us many useful objects such as wickerwork picnic baskets. Imagination without skill gives us modern art." Melding skill and imagination...now that is the key to great music.

Speaking of great music, in high school I became a devoted fan of the Grateful Dead, the original improvisational jam-band. Thankfully, my parents never seemed to mind loud music, as I loved to crank up the tunes and whistle along behind the closed door in my room. On long bike rides with buddies, we'd listen to the Dead from a cassette recorder nestled in a rear panier, and I'd whistle along with Jerry Garcia's meandering riffs. This was a critical period when I cracked open my repertoire and started to add other styles to my classical music regimen.

Over the years, whistling while biking and walking helped me develop exceptional breath control, which creates a smooth and constant sound. But smooth and constant doesn't always prevent quivers and shakes.

Freshman year in college, I had my biggest audience ever. I went from whistling for myself for the most part to performing in front of more than 500 people at a residential college talent show. I had prepared a medley of Billy Joel songs, starting with the whistled beginning of *The Stranger*, but I wasn't expecting to be so nervous.

Off stage with a cup of water in hand, I waited my turn. A group of fifteen or so women were finishing up a choreographed dance routine set to "Stray Cat Strut" by the rockabilly group the Stray Cats. Many thoughts ricocheted around my brain as I stood there. *Will I remember the order of the songs? Will they like it? Will my mouth get dry? Why am I doing this?!* No time for answers; up the stairs I went, to commence what would turn out to be the first of many whistling performances in front of large audiences.

Within moments of puckering and blowing, I noticed that one of my legs was shaking from the knee down. From the audience, it probably looked like I was keeping time with my foot. Then I detected a quivering lip in places I hadn't planned a vibrato. My nervous energy was looking to exit my body through the most convenient portals, and it was succeeding.

The show went on, and I controlled my nervousness enough to knock out a respectable Billy Joel tribute, though it was ironic that the last song in the medley was "Pressure!" People told me afterward that that was the first time they had ever heard a serious whistler in public…and that they liked it.

Curiously, a previous attempt to perform at a college talent show had been thwarted. The organizers rejected my proposed performance of *The Lone Ranger* song. They thought a whistler was unique, but that the audience wouldn't "get it."

A lame excuse, I thought, but a foreshadowing of what I would confront throughout my whistling career. To this day, there are some people who think whistling is fascinating, and others who are repulsed by the notion. How people will react is totally unpredictable; I've had musicians reject me and Wall Street executives embrace me.

I graduated from college in 1986 and took a two-part gap year. The first half, I was a waiter at a seafood restaurant on the eastern tip of Long island, living in a trailer park with friends. That's the summer I learned to love (and whistle) Beethoven's Ninth Symphony. Walking along the beach with my Sony Walkman, listening to his Ninth over and over, is emblazoned in my mind. Most people are familiar with the final choral movement, a catchy tune known as "Ode to Joy," but the preceding three movements are just as powerful and gorgeous.

The second half of my gap year, I was a ski bum in Idaho and Wyoming. I whistled while traversing the slopes, and had a delightful experience singing Handel's *Messiah* with a Mormon choir in Driggs, Idaho, a town near the Grand Targhee ski hill in Wyoming.

I moved to Washington, DC in early 1987, and started whistling at open mic nights, doing blues and jazz. Open mic nights are exciting and challenging. They are like pick-up football games in grade school. Sometimes you know the fellow players, sometimes you don't. Everyone has a position, but you haven't practiced together, and you may not even know the song well.

The human whistle is versatile. It can do the melody or improvise on the main themes. In a typical jazz piece, each instrument gets to shine: the piano, guitar, sax, and harmonica. By adding "whistler" to the list, I hoped to give the art more legitimacy.

Along those lines, a key challenge keeping whistling from gaining critical acceptance or credibility is that there is virtually no music written for a whistler. Sure, there's "Whistle While You Work" from *Snow White and the Seven Dwarfs*, and "I Whistle a Happy Tune" from the Broadway musical *The King and I*. On my CD, *The Symphonic Whistler*, is the song "On the Mall" by Edwin Franco Goldman, a song written for whistlers in 1927. There are a few others, but for the most part, the repertoire for lips is parched.

So, what's a whistler to do? We resort to covering songs written for other instruments. Also on my CD is Mozart's Oboe Concerto and Hummel's Trumpet Concerto. In those performances, I am the oboe and the trumpet. Sometimes I think I am the walrus, but then remember that the Beatles did not write any songs exclusively for whistlers.

One benefit of this approach is that if a familiar tune is rendered well with a different instrument (the whistle, in this case), then audiences can think, *Oh yeah, I know that song, and hearing it whistled was pretty cool.* And maybe they come away with a positive impression of whistling.

I became a regular at the Sunset Grille's open mic nights, where whistling was rare, but most people thought it was cool enough. Roger Edsel, a fantastic blues harmonica player, became my advocate. He saw the potential of the whistle from the first day we met, and made sure I got on stage to show my stuff.

Roger was a full-time dad and a musician on the side. I learned a lot by watching and listening to him perform. Thankfully, he was open to my many questions. When people ask how I got to be a good whistler, Roger is on the short list of those who influenced me and made me a better musician and performer. He's a balanced mix of intensity, gentleness, and joviality, sassy and kidding around one moment, but then fired up and focused the next.

When I had the chance to perform on the *Today Show* with Katie Couric, my first call was to Roger. He embraced the idea immediately and quickly put together a band. We performed an upbeat jump boogie tune. It was an amazing experience, one of my best TV appearances ever.

Jamming live on stage is exciting and challenging. Audience feedback lets you know what's working and what's not. There's give and take with fellow band members. Improvising live is so different from reading music or performing someone else's notes from memory. It's a great "in the moment" phenomenon. Everything is real time. You're hearing music from bandmates and yourself simultaneously. It's like driving around a corner at high speed in a sports car. You have some idea of what's coming, but not much notice. Speedy reflexes are a must.

Then things got serious.

In the fall of 1992, some friends and I were hiking Old Rag, one of the tallest peaks in the Shenandoah National Park in central Virginia. As usual, I was whistling some happy tune. A friend of a friend said, "Wow, you're a really good whistler. You should do something with it. Have you ever competed?"

I noted that I had once seen a whistler on *The Tonight Show* with Johnny Carson, but knew nothing else about competitive whistling.

The gears starting turning. *If there's a hog-calling contest, and a hollerin' contest, and countless other gatherings of like-minded subculturalists, there must be something for whistlers.*

Our mutual friend, Elizabeth Foster (formerly Sauer), said if a competition existed, she would find it. Back then there was no Internet, so Elizabeth delved deep into a directory of national events found in the library, and there it was: The National Whistlers Convention. It was an annual event hosted by the Franklin County Arts Council in Louisburg, North Carolina. In April 1993, they were planning the twentieth annual gathering, the highlight of which would be a competition.

Within weeks, I was registered, and began six months of preparations.

For twenty-five years, I had been *the whistler* in my home, community, college, and job. But I was soon to learn that other people had also earned that moniker. At home, we were lone stars, but in Louisburg, we became a constellation, burning brighter in the presence of kindred spirits.

The road trip from Washington to Louisburg took around four hours, and my stomach was in knots the whole way. Elizabeth was a great road trip partner, offering encouragement and keeping the mood focused on how crazy and freaky this was going to be.

With some trepidation, I got out of my car on the campus of Louisburg College and approached the building that housed the registration desk and concert hall where the competition would be held. It's a large red brick and glass building built in the 1980s, utilitarian and boring, but over the years I would come to view it fondly as the focal point and home for competitive whistling, which would dominate a large part of my waking hours for more than a decade.

Immediately, sounds emanating from puckered lips tickled my ears: scales and arpeggios and trills and songs and random notes. I had heard all these sounds before, but never together and never from so many other people. I was no longer alone in the desert. I had found my people.

Much to my delight, virtually everyone I met was courteous and welcoming. In sync with the image of whistling as a happy-go-lucky activity, the convention was friendly, fierce, and fair. Whistlers are a diverse group—old, young, male, female, straight, gay, happy, sad, sophisticated, naïve, urban, country. Whistlers from all over the world had gathered in the tiny town of Louisburg to learn new skills, meet fellow whistlers, and see who was the best.

In 1993, the competition consisted of three divisions: adults, teens, and kids. (A few years later, there was further division by gender, along with a seniors' category.) To vie for the grand championship, adults and teens had to compete in both the classical and popular categories.

I performed Glenn Miller's "In the Mood" in the popular category, and the finale of the *William Tell Overture* in the classical category. To my shock, I placed second in the popular category. On my inaugural run with the whistling big dogs, I realized I was able to keep up.

The next year, I won the grand championship, which unleashed my fifteen minutes of fame (though insanity is a better description). I earned additional first place grand champion titles in 1996, 1999, and 2000. In 2012, I was inducted into the International Whistling Hall of Fame, joining such whistling luminaries as Bing Crosby and Roger Whittaker.

Over the years, people have asked me how I got started and how I got to be a champion. Since I do marketing and public relations for a living, here's my talking point summary:

1. Ability to whistle: Thankfully, I inherited the gift of whistle—not everyone can do it. (I've also developed some funky techniques, which make me more versatile and differentiate me in competitions.)
2. Love of music: All kinds, all the time...it warms my heart and challenges my brain.
3. Great ear: I can reproduce what I hear in the right key and with good pitch.
4. Good arranger: I have the ability to arrange a song for lip.

5. Song selection: I'm good at picking songs that reflect my abilities and can wow the judges.
6. Relentless practice: I love to explore new approaches and then refine them.
7. Open to constructive criticism: Constant improvement is the key to success.
8. Competitive spirit: Competition brings out the best in my ability.

So, over the next twenty-three years—from my first victory in 1994 to the present—I've experienced my own version of the Grateful Dead's "long, strange trip." Mine just hasn't involved psychotropic drugs (though I am addicted to ChapStick, and have consumed mass quantities over the years).

It has been a wholly unexpected and completely unpredictable journey—astounding, actually. A childhood hobby has become an inextricable and defining part of my adult persona, life, and even my day job. Whistling has made my life better and richer and funnier. I've been able to go places and meet people and experience things and touch lives in ways that never would have been possible otherwise. In the early and mid-years, it was a parallel life, but in the past twenty years or so, it has become core to who I am, inextricable from the rest of me.

I am the Whistler, and this is how I became it.

CHAPTER 3
A Friendship Beyond Words

FOUR YEARS AFTER winning my fourth grand championship, I decided to come out of retirement and go for a five-peat. No one had won the grand championship five times, so there was great appeal to being the "winningest" whistler ever. I hoped to be like basketball great Michael Jordan and reclaim my crown.

At that point, 2004, I was fully ensconced in my career at Carlyle, a father of two, and attempting to be a worthy husband, brother, son, and friend, as well as exercise occasionally. Though I whistled daily, it was more for fun than improvement.

You may see where this is going.

I ended up tying for third place grand champion. In retrospect, it's clear what happened. My song selection was lackluster and I didn't rehearse enough. Life got in the way, and my hunger for winning had waned.

But in the end, I received a gift far greater than winning a fifth trophy (with the accompanying bragging rights) and claiming the $350 purse.

I learned what love truly is.

———

Two weeks before the competition, the *Washington Post* did a story on my upcoming attempt to reclaim my title. They came to Carlyle, took pictures, and wrote a fun and flattering story that appeared prominently in the Metro section of the paper.

A few days after the story appeared, I got a call from a stranger named Kathy who had seen the story and wanted to buy an autographed CD for her son's nineteenth birthday. Preston, Kathy told me, was a whistler too. In fact, it was one of the ways he communicated, because he was physically and developmentally challenged.

I told Kathy I was delighted to send her a signed CD, and asked when Preston's birthday was, so I could whistle for him. June 30, she said.

And thus was born a friendship like none other, though I didn't know it at the time.

In fact, once the CD was mailed and his birthday was recorded in my calendar, I didn't think about Preston again until the day before June 30, when I saw his name on my birthday whistle list.

Many people praise my amazing ability to "remember" so many birthdays. I always chuckle. "Trust me," I tell them, "it's nothing against you, but I barely remember anyone's birthday. If you want to be impressed with something, it's my diligence in putting the names on the list in the first place, and then actually whistling for them."

In a fun coincidence, Preston's last name is Ulman, with one "L." We are not related. I now refer to Preston and his family as the "One-L-Ulmans."

With some trepidation, I dialed the Ulmans on June 30. I'm a talker, and wasn't sure how to handle a situation where someone can't talk. Kathy answered the phone with a surprised and delighted greeting. She thanked me for calling and said she would get Preston.

She put us on speakerphone and introduced us.

"Hi Preston, this is Chris Ullman. Happy birthday! Your Mom told me that you like to whistle. I like to whistle too."

Then I was quiet.

And there it was—a gentle whisper of a whistle.

Preston Ulman was talking to me, responding to me, in the way that he knew and was able. It was beautiful.

I whistled a little in response. Immediately, I felt at ease.

Kathy chimed in and said that Preston was smiling. That made me smile.

After a little more chitchat, I asked if he was ready for his serenade, and Kathy said yes.

Inhaling, I closed my eyes and tried to picture this nineteen year-old young man sitting next to his loving mom. With lips pursed, I exhaled, and out came a celebration of Preston's life.

Though it was only a drop in the sea of love his family had given to him throughout his life, I was honored and excited to help the ocean rise a teeny bit.

I heard a response from Preston, a few sweet, high-pitched notes that said thanks for calling. Kathy expressed similar sentiment with words, and then we said goodbye.

I went on with my life and they went on with theirs, until June 30, 2005.

I called Preston again on his twentieth birthday. This time, his mom was more surprised than the previous year. We chatted for a few moments, and then she got Preston on the phone.

"Hi Preston. It's your whistling friend, Chris Ullman, calling to wish you a happy birthday." I told them a little about what was going on in my life and then whistled for him. It was a quick call.

Another year passed.

A few weeks before Preston's twenty-first birthday, Kathy called me, asking if I would be willing to come to his birthday party, which would be at his school, to meet the family, visit with Preston and his friends, and whistle some tunes.

"Sign me up," I said.

Preston had been attending St. Coletta, a school for children with intellectual disabilities, since he was around fifteen years old. Kathy gave me the address of the school, and I realized it was only three miles from my house; not only had I never heard of it, I had gone by it many times but never noticed.

There have been many moments in my life when I realized I live in a bubble of routines, norms, and privilege, but none as profound as this time.

I went to and from my job in DC five days a week, and spent much of the remaining time with my wife and children, squeezing in bike rides, occasionally visiting with friends, and hoping for a date with my wife every ten days or so.

My day job is the ultimate bubble. The people I work with are among the smartest around. My bosses are billionaires. As a corporate spokesman, I deal with top journalists at major news outlets every day. I go to gala events at the Kennedy Center for the Performing Arts where my boss, David Rubenstein, is the chairman, and Wolf Trap National Park for the Performing Arts, where my other boss, Dan D'Aniello, is the chairman. I do the PR for David Rubenstein's personal patriotic philanthropy, which has taken me from the pinnacle of the Washington Monument to the rarely seen basement of the Lincoln Memorial, and enabled me to meet Morley Safer of *60 Minutes* fame. I've even gotten up close with the famous pandas at the National Zoo, one of whom I hand-fed a breakfast biscuit. They also pay me well. If that's not a bubble, I don't know what is. I try to be humble and grateful, and we support many charities, but it's still easy to be ignorant of how other people live.

My world is not one of physical or mental infirmity. Mine is one of high-octane performance—do well, or someone else will do well in your place. That's the way it is in pretty much every job I've had. That's the deal, and everyone knows it.

For many years, I tutored and mentored in inner city Washington, which exposed me to many precious children besieged by dysfunctional families, poverty, and terrible schools. That helped get me out of my bubble, or at least pierce it a bit. Getting to know Preston and his family pulled me further outside my bubble.

Meeting for the first time was very special, like a homecoming. I felt like I knew everyone already, even though we hadn't met until Preston's birthday party. I was a little anxious at first, but everyone made me feel welcome. Kathy gave me a hug, and her more formal, bowtie-wearing husband Craig gave me a warm handshake. Preston's sister Libby was there as well.

Preston was seated around a table with several friends and classmates. Kathy introduced us. "Preston, this is your friend Chris Ullman. He's the whistler."

"Hi Preston," I said while reaching out to shake his hand. He didn't extend his hand, so I simply reached a little further, catching a few fingers and gently squeezed for a moment. It was nice to connect in person, to feel his warmth. Our eyes met for a moment, but he quickly looked away.

I whistled a few random notes so he could connect me with the previous phone calls. He smiled and responded with a few gentle notes of his own. I smiled and returned his volley.

We all put on pointed, rubber band-anchored birthday hats and started the festivities. I whistled an official "Happy Birthday" and then we feasted on cake.

Kathy, Craig, and I got better acquainted. I met Preston's classmates and teachers and whistled a few more tunes. Work was calling, so we hugged some and said our goodbyes. The visit lasted no more than forty minutes, but the memories are still fresh, eleven years later.

As I pulled out of the nearby parking spot, about to reenter my bubble world, I pledged to wonder more about the people and places around me.

It was a stark reminder of all that we don't know, all that we presume about people. You're on the subway, or a bus, or in line at Disney, and you're surrounded by strangers. We form conclusions based on hair, clothes, posture, ethnicity, skin color. It's all so risky and presumptuous. We know so little about those around us.

Sometimes when I'm with my billionaire bosses in public, I wonder if passersby realize they're standing next to someone with unimaginable amounts of money. Unless someone actually recognizes one of the bosses, there's no reason they'd know what they're worth. They don't wear lapel pins with dollar signs on them; they dress in normal business suits and they're pretty regular looking men in their sixties and seventies. Nothing screams, "Look at me, I'm rich, I'm in the top .001% of income earners."

So, sometimes we presume things about people because of how they look or act, and sometimes we miss things because they blend in. The real lesson is to get more information, to talk less and listen more. Two ears, two eyes, one mouth—there's a powerful ratio going on there, suggesting we should do more observing and less concluding and talking. I'm not claiming to have mastered this approach, but it's often on my mind, and I try to instill it in my children and remind myself to practice what I preach. On those times I drove by St. Coletta, I had no idea who was inside or what they were doing. Like passing an innocuous billionaire on the street, I was missing so much.

Once I was inside, a new world was opened to me. Inside are some pretty amazing people, fellow citizens whose lives are just as precious in God's eyes as mine, but who have challenges that many of us are unfamiliar with—challenges so intense and incredible that they'd make our knees buckle. But they and their similarly precious caregivers soldier on. They're doing what they do because that's what they do. It seems circular, and to some extent it is, but that's the beauty of embracing one's reality. You do what has to be done because there aren't many other options.

At Preston's birthday party, I didn't see a bunch of mopey people feeling sorry for themselves or seeking sympathy. I witnessed parents, caregivers, and kids having a good time, excited for Preston, hungry for ice cream and cake, eager for summer break, and maybe even a little fascinated by this bow-tie wearing stranger who was whistling some happy tunes.

I've had lots of applause over the years, but none was sweeter than that which came from Preston and his friends that day. It was unbridled, honest, unassuming, and joyful. I don't think it was necessarily me. I bet a talented kazoo player or a violinist with the National Symphony would have gotten the same reaction. It was a few moments of carefree joy. There was no worry or pain.

It reminded me of these perfect moments I'd have as a kid. With two dollars in my pocket, I'd ride my Schwinn Stingray a half-mile to Park Boulevard in downtown Massapequa Park and get a slice at Mario's Pizza, then go two doors down to DiMonda's Bakery for a chocolate and cherry homemade Italian ice.

My money, my bike, my alone time to think about life: it was nirvana. That feeling of peacefulness and fulfillment is still so powerful and comforting that I recreate the experience even today by getting in my car alone, driving to nearby Valentino's Pizza (great NY-style pizza), then chasing it down with a Baskin Robbins chocolate peanut butter cone.

I hope I don't sound like I'm mythologizing these moments. Whether it's serenading Preston and his friends or getting slices of pizza and frozen treats, these are indelible images and feelings. These are the moments that shape and guide us, give us energy, make us smile, and warm our hearts.

Speaking of warm hearts, a few years after meeting the Ulmans at St. Coletta, I was whistling at a senior citizens' home in Maryland, when who do I see in the audience but Preston's mom, Kathy. In addition to being about twenty-five years younger than most of the audience, Kathy's smile made her stand out. She had seen an ad in a community newspaper about my upcoming performance.

I so enjoy whistling for seniors. They are the generation that helped make whistling a phenomenon in the '40s and '50s. The music I like to whistle is also more in line with their interests. When I whistle for younger crowds, I'm often asked to do some Adele, Madonna, Britney Spears, or Beyoncé. That's when my face usually scrunches up, and I feel a little clueless and old. But I pivot quickly. "Sorry," I say, "I don't know that song, but how about some Duke Ellington, Beethoven, Brahms, or Glenn Miller?" Blank stares usually meet my hopeful offerings. At that point, I usually just launch into a song and try to let the power of the whistling trump the lack of familiarity.

Part of the challenge is that music performed a cappella, meaning without accompaniment, has to have a strong melody that can be carried by a one-note-at-a-time instrument, such as a whistler. A lot of modern music I find relies on the ensemble of instruments to create the sound and melody that fans are familiar with. So, even if I liked modern pop, I don't think it's that whistleable. Maybe I haven't tried enough.

Over the years, we've gotten to be friends with the Ulmans. They've taken us sailing on the Chesapeake. They come to our annual New Year's party, and we get together for lunch and dinner here and there.

An annual highlight is the gala fundraiser for the organization that supports Preston. It's a roast of some bigwig, such as former Redskins quarterback Joe Theismann or super sports agent David Falk. And while everyone is dressed up and looking good, the real stars of the night are the clients of Jubilee.

Jubilee Association of Maryland, a place brimming with love, enables people with physical and mental challenges to have a sweeter, more productive life as part of a community. Clients learn skills, make friends, and receive medical and other support.

Preston lives with his parents, but spends weekdays at a Jubilee home supported by a full-time aide. Like St. Coletta, I hadn't heard of Jubilee until introduced to it by the Ulmans.

As Kris and I made our way through the crowd, I knew I was in the right place. This wasn't a typical hoity-toity Washington party of just the beautiful, powerful, and well-connected. At those parties, you don't see people with Down Syndrome, others in wheelchairs, or folks like Preston who need aides by their side. Once again, I was reminded of how segregated our society is. It's not just blacks and whites who very much live and socialize apart from each other, though I see some progress in these areas. The able-bodied and disabled are also very much segregated.

Amidst the mob of Jubilee supporters, we finally found the Ulmans: Kathy, always so gracious and quick with a smile and a hug; Preston and his dad Craig decked out in bowties, as was I.

I hugged Preston and met his caregiver Rebecca. Preston and I whistled a little for each other and I looked into his eyes and he smiled. Then a precious thing happened. Preston reached for my hand and simply held it. He was now flanked on his right by Rebecca and on his left by me. I had never experienced something like this before. I kept assuming he would let go, but he didn't. Holding hands with men at parties isn't my thing. Heck, holding hands with women who aren't my wife or daughters at parties isn't my thing either. Handshakes are supposed to last a prescribed amount of time. Too little time spent grabbing and it seems furtive, and too much time spent gripping and it becomes uncomfortable.

There we were, the fifty-two year-old PR guy and the thirty year-old wordless handicapped man, holding hands amidst a sea of people who were spending their evening and their money celebrating the beauty and dignity of all of God's children, regardless of ability. It took me a little while to get comfortable, but I did, and it was nice. It was a simple way for us to communicate, to show our caring and love.

As a professional communicator, I am wed to the written and spoken word. If I were a carpenter, they would be my pine and nails. They are indispensable. But are they enough? Does an overreliance on words mask simpler and deeper means of communicating? Thinking back to that first birthday serenade delivered via phone to a faceless presence, I never could have imagined that I would learn to communicate with Preston. But he has taught me that you work with what you've got—a smile, a whistle, a touch, a gaze. And what's nice is that Preston's parents let us figure this out on our own.

In 2013, I did a whistle-talk at the TEDx Mid Atlantic conference in Washington, DC. My concluding story was about meeting Preston and his family, and how much I had learned from them. I spoke of some of the challenges they faced as a family, but it wasn't about feeling sorry for them. It was about appreciating how they managed their trials with grace and quiet strength. In the end, I was the one given a gift: the chance to see unconditional love in action. How rare, how unexpected, how uplifting.

Preston's father Craig was in the audience that day. Having him there, representing his family, made my storytelling come alive. I got a standing ovation that day, but I think they were really honoring Preston and his family.

A *Whistle* That Touches My Heart

Name: Frances Ullman
Home: Alexandria, VA
Job: My mom
Fran's *Whistle*: Empathy
How I Know Fran: We met on May 9, 1963 at 3:16 p.m. in the delivery room of Peck Memorial Hospital in Brooklyn, NY, though I have no recollection of the blessed event.

***Whistle* in Action**: In our kitchen growing up hung a plaque: "Great Spirit, grant that I may not criticize my neighbor until I have walked a mile in his moccasins." That well captures my mother's spirit of empathy, which pervades her thoughts and deeds. It's as if her own challenging childhood gave her a window into the hidden struggles that so many of us have. When my siblings and I complained of annoying grade school classmates, mom's response was universally: "Be nice to them, they have problems at home." Though the response itself was frustrating to a pre-teen seeking validation of grievances, over time it seeped into my soul. Today when I show compassion to someone in need, it's my mom's heart and love I'm channeling. Her empathy is so simple, but so mind-bogglingly deep. It comes from a complex place I will never fully comprehend; it manifests itself in ways that are obvious and devoid of rationale, as pure love should be; it is instinctual, joyous. Because of her I try hard to ask questions and listen to the answers; I've learned to extend a hand rather than a finger; I've seen that the journey is better if the shoes I'm wearing aren't always mine.

CHAPTER 4
Louisburg: The Whistling Capital of the World

FOR NEARLY A HALF CENTURY, a wisp of a city in North Carolina has earned the title of whistling capital of the world. Louisburg's 3,500 residents reside around thirty miles north of the famous Research Triangle. The main drag through town is dotted with fast food joints, a few hotels, gas stations, and convenience stores.

Off the beaten path, in April, around the time of the International Whistlers Convention, there are azaleas—thousands of them, red and pink and white, robust and pretty, nurtured by people who adore lovely things. Other than seeing whistling friends and competing for the crown, the azaleas were my favorite part of trekking to Louisburg eleven times (nine as a competitor and two as a judge).

People are often amused when I tell them that this international event is in a tiny town. Perhaps they imagine puckered competitors basking in the grandeur of Carnegie Hall's main stage, or the Kennedy Center's concert hall. Over the years, many people have asked me if it's the same town where the National Hollerin' Contest takes place. Puh-leez! No, that's Spivey's Corner, also in North Carolina. It's unclear why people conflate whistling and hollerin'. I suspect it's because there's a part of the brain that stores odd activities that people do with their mouth. I got over it years ago. Now I find it humorous, another window into the human condition.

The event takes place on the grounds of Louisburg College, a small private two-year college with roots stretching back to the late 1700s. Most of the action occurs in the Seby B. Jones Performing Arts Center, a rather utilitarian auditorium that seats around 600. I was a little shocked the first time I went to the convention in 1993. Back then, the historic downtown was mostly run-down, with a few sad looking shops and cheap eateries. One year in a consignment shop, my mom and friend Elizabeth Foster, who had joined me on the road trip, discovered a two-foot tall statue of Jesus clad in beige velvet. Instantly, a battle cry was found: "Velvet Jesus!" uttered with a requisite Southern drawl. Over the years, "Velvet Jesus" has been a code phrase between the three of us when reminiscing about our many trips to Louisburg.

Why Louisburg? The real question is how did a whistling convention stay vibrant for forty years? The simple answer is: Allen De Hart, a man who couldn't even whistle, never made a penny for his countless hours of effort, and had to deal with lots of grief from whiny whistlers. He did it for fun, for community, to foster joy, and he succeeded, in buckets, in deluges, in fusillades.

Allen was a long-haul kind of guy. He was forty-eight at the first whistling competition, and turned ninety in 2016. (He died in October 2016 as I was completing this book.) A literal manifestation of his long-term perspective on life was his love of the Appalachian Trail. When he wasn't creating a forum for the world's best whistlers to convene and compete, he became one of the foremost experts on the 2,200-mile trail, writing numerous books and articles on its twists and turns, flora and fauna.

While he didn't necessarily set out to create a whistling institution, through Southern charm-infused doggedness, he did just that over nearly half a century. Allen was director of public affairs at Louisburg College in the late 1960s to 1980s. He organized a folk festival in 1970 that morphed into a talent show, which was subsumed by the whistling convention and competition starting in 1974.

Slight of build with a charming Southern accent, wry smile, and calculating eagerness, Allen was an organizational tour de force. Over the years he built an institution, knitting together an army of public and private sector advocates, volunteers, funding sources, and most importantly, whistlers. Since inception, the competition has been structured pretty much the same, with some tweaks to accommodate growing interest and (I believe) political correctness. In the years I first competed, there were three age groups: kids, teens, and adults. A few years in, the adults and teens were divided by gender. For the adults, that change was driven by the dearth of women winning awards. I was not a fan of this change, because gender has nothing to do with one's ability to whistle. Range, pitch, technical prowess, and initiative are not linked to gender. My opinion was not solicited, and, as a regular prize winner, my views probably would have been suspect anyhow.

For the adults, a preliminary round winnows the field in half or slightly more, followed by the finals, with possible whistle-offs in the case of ties. They happen more than you might think and the competitors would hope. I was in three whistle-offs over the years. My most intense whistle-off was captured on film in 2004, the last year I competed, and featured in the documentary *Pucker Up: The Art of Fine Whistling*. It was the year I was hoping to reclaim my title, last won in 2000.

After winning back-to-back championships (1999 and 2000), I was barred from competing for two years. That was pretty lame; imagine telling Tiger Woods he couldn't play in the Masters Golf Tournament because he had won it too many times. Anyhow, with the birth of our second child in April of 2003, I was overwhelmed at home and decided to not compete that year as well. So, 2004 was the year I was aiming to win an unprecedented fifth title. I tied for third place, but not before a dramatic whistle-off against a first-time competitor from the Netherlands.

There are three categories that adults can compete in: classical, popular, and allied arts. To vie for grand champion status, adults must perform in the classical and popular divisions. Allied arts, which does not count toward the grand championship and is therefore less stressful, brings together whistling plus another activity, such as dancing, piano, even parents. My mom and dad attended several of the competitions, and each performed with me once in the allied arts category. My father and I did "Dueling Banjos," from the movie *Deliverance*. It was very special to whistle with my dad, the man who'd taught me how to pucker and blow. Another year, my mom and I performed "Mama Tried" by Merle Haggard, popularized by the Grateful Dead. Not being a whistler, she held up funny signs while I puckered away. I competed in allied arts for several years, until I realized it was a distraction and focused all of my energies on winning the classical and popular categories.

Four judges award points based on three groups of criteria: technical ability (key, pitch, range, etc.), interpretive ability (arrangement of the piece and artistry), and stage presence. I was a judge in 2011 and 2013, and now have a better appreciation for the challenges professional sports umpires and judges face. If you do a good job, no one even notices you. If you screw up, you're the turd in the punchbowl; everybody blames you for their favorite team or athlete losing. That said, there's great satisfaction, even honor, in trying to give every performer your undivided attention, apply the rules fairly, and treat everyone equally.

In the eleven times I competed or judged, the gaggle of fifty or so competitors was always an odd mish-mash of ability. The bell curve was on full display: By my estimates, ten percent of the whistlers were terrible and shouldn't have been in the event; thirty percent were a little better than people you hear whistling on the street; fifty percent were very good to excellent; and ten percent were the best in the world.

Part of the challenge with the process of crowning the world's best whistlers is that there are no regional or preliminary competitions that lead up to the annual international convention and competition in Louisburg. There's no marketing budget; it's effectively a word-of-mouth enterprise that relies on the winners to secure free media attention to get the word out about whistling in general and the competition in particular.

First-time applicants are required to submit a demo tape of their whistling. Allen De Hart told me over the years that he'd rejected countless terrible whistlers based on the demo tape alone. That's comforting, but not fully persuasive. I suspect there was a need to reach a critical mass of attendees and competitors to keep the event exciting and substantial; an international competition with only five to seven competitors would not work well. You also never know when a dark horse will appear and wins hearts, minds, and trophies, as Geert Chatrou did in 2004.

For me, the whistling competition was always a love-hate proposition—intense periods of rehearsal, leading up to days of gut-churning nerves, followed by either rapturous victory or frustrating defeat. Internally, it was quite an emotional rollercoaster. Externally, I worked hard to stay balanced and even-keeled. The seeds for this approach were sown early in my life. Growing up, I played a lot of baseball and tried hard to win, but never collapsed in tears or hated myself if I lost a game. My father's perennial question upon learning of a loss was: "Did you try your hardest?" He was less impressed by victory at all cost and more interested in hard work and skill maximization. *Did I use the gifts God had given me to the fullest extent...or did I fritter them away?* This way of thinking had a profound effect on me growing up, and has carried over to how my wife and I teach and motivate our three children.

All that said, I do like to win. Taking first place in the 1994 competition triggered in me some latent ferocity that propelled me through many years of competing. Even I was surprised, as I don't consider myself a classic type-A win-at-all-cost/tunnel-vision kind of person. I give myself a type-A-minus grade in the intensity department. After one victory, the prospect of winning was an amazing motivator. That's the only way I was able to rehearse the same pieces over and over for months at a time and not go bonkers.

I've long been fascinated by people who love obscurity and work hard to stay there, versus those who love the limelight and work hard to get there. Allen De Hart fell squarely in this former category. Best

I can tell, his satisfaction came from serving, not from winning. He certainly found his *whistle*, and a key part of his *whistle* is forbearance. In my mind, over the years, I've thought *Poor Allen De Hart* a hundred times. With what he had to put up with from aggrieved whistlers, you'd have thought the purse was $1 million, rather than the $300 to $500 the organizers could muster. Then I remembered human nature.

For many people, it's not about the money; it's about ego, principle, precedent, bragging rights, or a dozen other rationales for creating a fuss. They claimed that the rules were complex, unclear, and unfair, and the organizers and judges were biased against old people, women, hand whistlers, slow and pretty whistlers, newcomers, and non-Americans. At the time, I believed these claims were unsubstantiated, and in the intervening years, I never heard any compelling evidence to change my mind.

One perennial complaint was that fast and technical whistlers have an edge over slow and pretty whistlers because flash trumps substance. This has always bothered me, as I'm known for being a fast and technical whistler. Simply put, it's a misconception that judges are directly comparing the two types of whistlers. How dog shows judge and name winners is effectively the same as how champion whistlers are chosen. Think of the best in show category at the finale of the Westminster Kennel Club Dog Show. In 2016, the seven finalists for best in show were dogs from the following breeds: Borzoi, Shih Tzu, Bulldog, German Shepherd Dog, Pointer, Samoyed, and Skye Terrier. It was quite a range of breeds.

So, how does a judge compare a large dog with a small dog? A short-hair with a long-hair? A hyper personality with a mellow demeanor? Simply put, they don't. Here's the secret: the judge determines to what extent each of the breeds comes closest to the ideal for *its* breed. The dog that is the best representation of its breed is the winner. Big doesn't trump small; hyper doesn't trump mellow, etc.

Like dogs, whistlers come with their own techniques, strengths, weaknesses, and preferences. I'm drawn to fast pieces with technically challenging runs that require fast tongue control and great rhythm. Meanwhile, other whistlers prefer soft and sweet songs that emphasize long soaring notes, smooth vibrato, and incredible breath control. The best whistlers migrate back and forth to ensure a wide skill set and repertoire. Geert Chatrou, arguably the best whistler in the world, blends fast and slow and blazing technical prowess in the songs he performs.

In my many years of competing, many of my songs were up-tempo. In 1999, I won the pop division with "Go Daddy-O" by Big Bad Voodoo Daddy. It's a brass-heavy big band song that allowed me to reach deep into my whistling bag of tricks, including liberal use of the "wa-wa" and "referee" whistles, funky techniques that I developed. The second year I competed, in 1994, I won the pop division with "This Nightlife," a rollicking country swing song by Clint Black. A few years later, I did "The Arrival of the Queen of Sheba" by G.F. Handel. It's a super-fast baroque standard that most people have heard but probably don't know the name.

But what about "slow" pieces? I love adagios, those languorous pieces that stroke your heart more than they excite the brain. Much of this book has been written while listening to mellow Beethoven, particularly the middle (or slow) movements of his five piano concertos. They put me in the mood without defining the mood, allowing me to write what I need to without feeling distracted or directed.

In 1999, I performed a slow and dreamy violin piece by the wonderful American composer Amy Beach, called "Invocation for Violin." Beach is probably the best female American composer (1867-1944) whom no one's ever heard of. I first learned about Beach when singing with the Capitol Hill Choral Society. Our conductor, Betty Buchanan, a musicologist and devotee of Beach, compiled an exquisite collection of her pieces, primarily choral, that we recorded, some for the first time ever. "Invocation for Violin" was the only instrumental piece on the CD; I fell in love with it instantly and hoped to one day perform it. It's a gorgeous song that packs an emotional punch.

As I prepared to reclaim my crown in 1999 after a two-year drought, I was looking for a passionate adagio, a piece laden with pining and emotion. My goal was to show that I was quite capable of performing *and* winning with a slow-tempo piece. I put a lot of work into my rehearsals, trying to get inside Beach's head to see what points she was making with this delicate yet strong violin piece. The piece reminds me of U.S. President Teddy Roosevelt's philosophy of speaking softly and carrying a big stick. The solo violin pleads its case high above, while the orchestra provides momentum that sweeps the main themes along, like a swift-moving river propelling a boat forward, never dominating the music (or swamping the boat!).

Though I felt good about my performance, I was pleasantly surprised when I won the classical division. It was comforting to know that I wasn't a one-trick pony and could win across musical genres. The critics? Well, we all know that critics enjoy being critical, so while some realized what I had accomplished, others hardly noticed and continued their attacks on us fast and technical whistlers.

Unrelated to the competition, a sweet bookend experience happened a few years later. I got to perform "Invocation for Violin" with the Las Colinas Symphony located in the suburbs of Dallas. To "be the violin" as the orchestra carried me away was an exquisite experience.

———————

Every great movement has a commander—in this case, Allen De Hart—but without ground troops, they are powerless. Year after year, Allen assembled a remarkable group of volunteers. By his side through most of the conventions was Lillian Benton. As quiet as Allen is loquacious, Lillian is the ultimate worker bee—head down, detail-oriented, efficient, and effective. With close-cropped white hair and a ruddy complexion, Lillian was a comforting presence through the many years I competed and judged. When Lillian was on the scene, you knew the job would get done. (It was a delight to see Lillian at Allen's funeral. Many sweet memories of those eleven visits to Louisburg flooded my brain and heart.)

There were many others who gave up countless hours of their

personal time to keep the whistling flame alive and bright: the folks who picked up whistlers at the local airport; people who opened their homes to strangers toting high hopes and ample supplies of lip balm; the mayor of Louisburg, who dutifully came every year, hoping for a boost to the local economy; the local Baptist pastor, who welcomed whistlers into his sacred Sunday service the day after the competition; the man who dressed up as Ben Franklin every year to entertain guests and competitors; the president of Louisburg College, who greeted the whistlers and their supporters to his campus; the perennial emcee of the event, Mitch Hider, himself a former champion whistler, who brought wit and storytelling vigor to his duties.

Then there were the whistlers themselves. From the moment I stepped foot on the Louisburg campus in April of 1993, I entered a new world, a place where I felt welcome and understood. It's a world my wife eventually dubbed a "sub-subculture." She's right. I just wish I had found it sooner. Across the board, I found the whistlers of Louisburg, regardless of nationality or language or ability or sexual preference, to be the nicest, most gracious, loving, and opinionated group of people I've ever encountered. Yes, the competition was the highlight, but as Allen De Hart regularly reminded participants, it was a convention first, a gathering of people with a common interest for the purpose of fellowship, sharing, and learning. It must have sunk in. Unlike the time ice skater Tanya Harding had her ruffian boyfriend crack rival Olympic ice skater Nancy Kerrigan in the knee with a club, no whistlers have ever hit a competitor in the lips or put glue in someone's ChapStick!

This fine spirit was immediately evident at the whistling school I attended on the first day of the 1993 convention. I had no idea what to expect, as this was the deep end of the pool. Like pretty much everyone there, I was coming from a hometown where I was THE whistler. Growing up in Massapequa Park on Long Island, in college at Binghamton, and then in Washington, DC, no one whistled as well as me. Perhaps that's because hardly anyone whistled. Now I was amidst some of the best whistlers in the world. It was unnerving and exciting, but I quickly realized I wasn't the only newcomer, and that my pucker could hold its own amidst more seasoned lips...at least those who were attending the whistling school. And most importantly, everyone—newcomers and old-timers alike—were ready to share and learn.

That first whistling school, taught by Mitch Hider, imparted all sorts of tips, from how the competition worked to how to warble like a champion.

In retrospect, those early Louisburg years were when I started to realize that my literal whistle was also a figurative *whistle*. With every conversation, jam session, and performance, I sensed that my whistle was a special gift that was going to do unexpected things and expose me to new experiences. At the convention and in competition, then at home through work and play, I began to see how whistling was a tool, a means to bring joy to hearts and music to ears. Through people like Allen De Hart and Lillian Benton, both non-whistlers, I also started to better understand and appreciate that everyone has a *whistle*, even if they can't pucker and blow.

There's a type of person whose *whistle* is giving and loving selflessly—people who volunteer as class parents at their kids' school, or serve as Scout leaders, or coach sports teams, or, in the case of Elizabeth Foster, manage a budding whistler's career.

Elizabeth and I met at Citizens for a Sound Economy, a free-market citizen advocacy group, in Washington in 1992. We hit it off right away and became close friends. I didn't fully realize it at the time, but without Elizabeth's support, encouragement, and love, I would not have accomplished anywhere near what I have in my whistling career, and possibly none of it. Without a solid foundation, nothing of substance can be built that will survive the test of time. Elizabeth helped me build that foundation, brick by brick.

After finding the convention, she helped me prepare for the competitions, critiquing song choices and techniques. She joined me at the first five or so conventions in Louisburg, providing invaluable moral support and confidence. She was a constant and trusted advisor on all things whistling, her judgment always spot-on. She made heartfelt keepsake photo albums. She helped make victories sweeter and defeats tolerable, and through it all, she was fun. We had great times road-tripping to Louisburg, gossiping about the quirky people we encountered, and making fun of ourselves when we took things too seriously. She even tried to get ChapStick to consider using me in their advertising.

Elizabeth has certainly found her *whistle*. She's a giver of time, love, and joy. She's one of those people who gets things done, always behind the scenes. It's not the limelight she craves, but the satisfaction of having made a difference—and what a difference she made in my life. I will be forever grateful for how she used her *whistle* to help me find and develop mine.

There's a hilarious scene in the documentary *Pucker Up: The Art of Fine Whistling* that depicts a whistle-off between Geert Chatrou and me at the 2004 competition.

The judges announced that there was a tie between the two of us that would be decided by a whistle-off. *Good news*, I thought. Geert had delivered superb performances the previous two days, so this meant he and I were running neck and neck.

The documentary cameras caught Geert and his wife outside the performance hall, strategizing on what song he should do in the whistle-off, all the while puffing away on cigarettes. At first, he contemplated doing "Bohemian Rhapsody" by Queen, his brief riff showing how talented he was. Then he decided to do the U.S. national anthem, hoping that a patriotic song would curry favor with the audience and judges, maybe even make them cry. The unrehearsed scene well captured Geert's wit and charm.

Meanwhile, away from the cameras, I was in the competitors' dressing room, pondering my options. I could have used one of the songs I had prepared for a tie-breaker, or reprised one of the songs I did in the competition, which the judges had said was permissible. I chose the latter approach, and got out the CD containing "Luck Be a Lady," from the musical *Guys and Dolls*, which had gone well in the final round. After running through it quickly, I headed backstage and prepared for the show-down.

Geert went first. Because I was backstage pacing and praying, I didn't see what happened when he performed "The Star Spangled Banner," but you can see it in the documentary. Geert's reaction was priceless. As the first notes of the national anthem left his lips, the audience of several hundred people rose, ball caps were removed, and hands were placed on hearts. Geert was startled by the commotion, his eyes lighting up, while his lips maintained their composure. It was a strong rendition of the U.S. national anthem, particularly by a non-American.

I heard the sustained applause and knew I had my work cut out for me. Two times in the past, tie scores had led to whistle-offs, where I was one-for-two. This time I was feeling good, so I planned on making it two-for-three.

"And now we have Chris Ullman of Alexandria, Virginia, who will perform 'Luck Be a Lady,'" said emcee Mitch Hider.

I walked out on stage as Mitch introduced me. Taking the microphone off the stand, I acknowledged the audience then nodded to the sound man, who started my musical accompaniment.

Moist and puckered, I pounced as the big brass sounds erupted out of the auditorium speakers. Knowing this would probably be the last time I ever performed in the international whistling competition, I was on fire from the get-go. *This is already fun*, I thought, acutely aware that whether or not I won an unprecedented fifth title would rest on this performance.

I used every technique in my whistling bag o' tricks: wa-wa whistle, referee whistle, warbles, slurs, glissandos. I whistled sucking in and blowing out. It was a symphony of sound and technique, my tongue and lips in perfect harmony, producing an even better rendition than the one earlier in the day.

With a fist pump in the air, the last notes left my lips. The audience was rapturous, its reaction reflecting how I'd performed and felt. With a bow and wave, I departed from the world of competitive whistling. After nine years on stage at Louisburg, I was done.

With my one year-old son in my lap and my wife and three year-old daughter by my side, I eagerly awaited the results. Mitch Hider came on stage and worked his way through the awards. After what seemed like an eternity, he announced that for the popular category, Geert had come in second place and I was first place. My heart jumped, knowing that even if I hadn't come in first in the classical category, my combined score could still make me the first place grand champion.

Then Mitch announced the classical winners. Geert was on top, and I didn't place or show. It took a moment for reality to sink in, but my hopes for a five-peat had been dashed. I ended up tying for third place grand champion. Steve Herbst, another long-time Louisburg competitor, came in second, and Geert was named first place grand champion. He deserved it.

———

As I was writing this chapter, I called Allen De Hart. He was home recuperating from surgery. We caught up and reminisced a bit. He told me of a museum that will be built on property he donated to the town of Louisburg. The museum will feature mementos from his many years running the convention. Even at ninety, his *whistle* was loud and clear; every day a chance to make a difference.

My in-laws live in Charlotte, North Carolina. At least twice a year, we make the eight-hour drive to visit them. On Interstate 85, soon after entering the state from Virginia, we come upon the Louisburg exit. Every time, I point it out to whomever in the car may be listening: "Hey, there's the Louisburg exit."

For me, it's like the door in the back of the closet in C.S. Lewis' *The Lion, The Witch and The Wardrobe*. It's a portal to another world. In my case, a place made special by remarkable people and precious memories, including Velvet Jesus.

Louisburg changed my life. Yes, the trophies and titles are nice, but the convention and competition taught me a lot about myself, helped me to grow up and realize what's important. Most importantly, it showed me how to make the most of the gifts I have been given. Through Louisburg, I found my *whistle*.

A *Whistle* That Touches My Heart

Name: Rocky Orfila
Home: Alexandria, VA
Job: Personal services business: Pet/house/babysitting
Rocky's *Whistle*: Giving spirit
How I Know Rocky: In 2004, our eldest daughter was in a pre-school program at the First Baptist Church in Alexandria, VA. Rocky, the daughter of our daughter's teacher, would babysit the little kids on parents' night out.

***Whistle* in Action**: For years, on the mornings of our three kids' birthdays, before dawn and long before any relative had called to offer a song or well wishes, Rocky Orfila would have already stealthily dropped off a package of treats by our front door. Rocky has a giving spirit that is second to none. She's generous with her time and good spirit, never complaining, always cheery. Several times, she volunteered to watch the kids overnight so Kris and I could take trips to New York City to catch Broadway plays. At one of our annual house parties, though she was technically a guest, she supervised the gaggle of kids eager to try the zip-line in our backyard. A Pokémon devotee, Rocky spent countless hours with our three kids teaching them the intricacies of the cards and game. Without Rocky, for years there would have been no date night, the frequent outings that helped Kris and I have a stronger, happier marriage. We knew she was special when our kids asked us to go out so Rocky could come over. Over a decade, Rocky's regular presence and giving spirit made a huge impact on our family that will always be remembered and appreciated.

CHAPTER 5
Happy Birthday: I'm Glad You Were Born

"OH DARN, I shouldn't have picked up."

That's generally not what you want to hear from a friend when you call.

"I was hoping to get it on the voicemail."

From a feelings standpoint, what's worse: someone picks up when I call and regrets it, or doesn't pick up and lets the serenade go to voicemail…every time? There are some people I haven't talked to in years on their birthdays because they want the voicemail. I got an e-mail from a buddy the other day saying he now has five consecutive renditions of "Happy Birthday" saved on his cell phone.

It took some getting used to. Now I know it's not personal!

"No problem," I say if someone answers, "How about I whistle live now and then call back and leave a voicemail?"

Most people feel bad about having me whistle twice, but I'm happy to do it. I'm especially tickled when someone isn't sheepish and wants a live rendition *and* a recorded version.

Whatever makes people happy is fine by me. In fact, I think it's hilarious.

"Are you a good networker?" asked a woman I met at a business lunch when I worked in the George W. Bush administration as the White House budget spokesman.

I had never been asked the question, so I had to pause and figure out my answer. It came to me pretty quickly, and more than fifteen years later, I feel the same way. The answer is yes. I'm drawn to people in general, and I like to keep in touch with people I find nice and intellectually engaging. If we can eventually help each other, then great, but that's not the point. Reveling in the beauty, dignity, and uniqueness of people—the greatest of God's creatures—is what it's all about.

Over the years, as I've moved from home to college and then from job to job in the real world, I've developed many wonderful friends and acquaintances. Whistling "Happy Birthday" has helped me keep in touch with people, even relatives, whom I otherwise might have drifted apart from through time and distance. The Whistlegram, as I call it, is a delightfully sticky glue that connects me to people, bringing continuity across the decades. It's a key that allows me to enter into someone's heart on his or her special day, and I get to do it 400 times a year. Sometimes I stop and think about how sweet that is, how blessed I am that the whistle gives me license to do that. If you think about it, in most cases, I otherwise would not be welcome. Sure, your closest friends and family typically expect some kind of greeting on their birthdays, a card or call. But you don't have to move too far beyond that group of intimates to have an unexpected birthday greeting seem a little odd, despite the good intent. The whistle, on the other hand, allows me to slip right in.

What is a birthday, when you get right down to it? Beyond the obvious marking of time, it's a celebration of life, an opportunity to revel in oneself or another, a time to reflect (especially on landmark birthdays), a reason to eat, drink, and be merry, and a reminder to give thanks, because life is the most precious gift of all. Without it, nothing else is possible.

At the core, birthdays are a great equalizer. No matter who you are or what you do, it's your day and it's special and no one can take it away. I know, because I've whistled for them all. I've serenaded the chief of staff to the president of the United States on his birthday, and turned around and whistled for an inner city kid on his special day. I've whistled for billionaires and centenarians and handicapped kids and intimates and strangers. For each, the whistle sent the same message: you are special, your life has value, the world is better because you are here.

Birthdays are so different from other holidays. A birthday is your day, your entrance into this world, this amazing, crazy, tragic, inspiring world. Even if you share the day with a sibling or friend, it's still yours. They're just a part of your special birthday club. I have a six-person birthday club. It includes John Ashcroft, former U.S. Attorney General whom my wife used to work for; friends Michelle Ong and Ted Wright; Hanna, the daughter of an American Airlines ticket agent who helped me one day in 2016 while picking my son up at the airport; and piano man Billy Joel, though he doesn't know he's a member. [Yes, I love his music, but I also feel a special bond with him because of May 9. So much so that when I was around seventeen, my friend Rob Siegel and I bicycled from our homes on the south shore of Long Island to Billy Joel's house on the north shore of the island. We stood outside the gates to his mansion and sang "Happy Birthday." (I hadn't started whistling "Happy Birthday" at that point.) There is no evidence he heard us.] On May 9, Michelle and I call each other and acknowledge "our" birthday and make lunch plans. It's fun. It's a club that meets once a year, and then we typically don't see each other for another year.

The whistle enables me to be a part of someone's special day, 400 times a year. It's like eating ice cream every day. It's a constant source of joy, an IV of happiness. I never grow tired of it. On those days I don't have a birthday whistle, I feel a little empty. At the rate I'm going, though, I'll have at least one birthday per day soon enough.

Yesterday, I delivered four birthday whistles, one each to Russell,

Henny, Jenny, and Theresa. Each of them, a former colleague, a long-term journalist friend, and two other long-term buddies, is special to me. They are unique children of God who wow me with their talent, insight, faith, and generosity. Whistling for Henny is always a bit of a challenge, as her job frequently takes her to Asia. Sometimes I get her live, other times I leave a voicemail, and then at some odd hour I get an e-mail thanking me. No matter where Henny is the world, and no matter who she happens to be with, she knows she'll get a serenade on her special day.

Maybe all this birthday whistling is weird. For those who know me well, they're probably nodding their heads right now, saying, "Yup, he's different, always has been." But imagine dozens of people every year saying "You made my day," after getting a birthday serenade. It sometimes makes me cry, like when I whistle for old folks facing the twilight.

Take Jean, for example. I met her at my Godmother Helen's (aka Chickie) funeral in 2010. When my wife, kids, and I met Jean, she already knew who everyone was.

"You must be Helen's Godson," her practiced New York accent turning God into Gawd. It brought back lots of memories of my youth on Long Island and college at Binghamton University, where a plurality of students came from Long Island.

"And this must be Justus," she added upon meeting our son. Who knows how many times Chickie had told her about us or shared school pictures with Jean over the years?

Like old friends, we reminisced and swapped Chickie stories. I was moved by her warmth, and sad that her best friend was gone, something, I suspect, she felt more acutely than us family because of their daily interaction. At lunch after the funeral, I asked for her birthday so I could whistle for her.

Now every August 23, I whistle for Jean. Two years ago, I got her live, rather than leaving a voicemail, as I had in most previous years. She had recently undergone surgery and was recuperating at home, so she couldn't leave the house on her birthday. I asked how she was doing, and she said I was the first person to talk to her that day. It wasn't eight in the morning. It was early afternoon. We chitchatted for a few minutes, and then I whistled for her. She said, "You made my day." I got off the phone and was quiet for a moment as her words sunk in.

You made my day.

It was a stark reminder that each of my 400 yearly "Happy Birthday" serenades is a celebration of a unique life. I'm not curing cancer, but I am delivering a little bit of love and caring to friends and strangers near and far.

You made my day. It lifts my heart every time. One good buddy tells me that his mom and I are the only ones who consistently call him on his birthday. He's a rather pragmatic and unemotional guy, so I don't think he gives a hoot that few people acknowledge his birthday. While nothing compares with a mom's birthday greetings, he definitely gets a kick out of the whistle; being acknowledged, even if it's not sought out, is comforting.

No matter how much I enjoy my day job, touching people's hearts gives me psychic benefit and energy that I never could have imagined. And it's helped to nurture a wonderful network of friends and acquaintances that enriches my life.

At the rate I'm going, and if I live until at least eighty, I've got another 12,000 "Happy Birthdays" to go. Each one is special, a moment to pause and celebrate life. What a gift I have been given!

Yesterday, I saw a mom at the airport pushing her kid in a stroller, which had a baby car seat hanging off the handle, while her free hand pulled a roller suitcase, and a stuffed backpack hung from her shoulders. While I was amazed how she managed, her face showed no stress, just determination. Through practice and process, it was just another day of motherhood.

Practice and process are my saving graces as well. The only way to whistle for so many people is to impose a military-like regimentation. If they were tangential to my daily rituals, I'd have crashed and burned long ago. Joy must be at the heart of it all, because without joy, I should just hang up my ChapStick and let Hallmark do the talking for me. It's a labor of love that makes me smile and chuckle virtually every day.

So far, so good. With 400 serenades per year, that's an average of 1.1 per day. Though I've got some days with no whistles, I have a bunch with three, several with four, three with five, and one day, June 19, with seven birthday serenades. That's a fun day. The key challenge is to make sure that each serenade is special and it never becomes a chore. An uninspired birthday serenade would be a missed opportunity.

Those heavy volume days require the most planning, especially if I'm on a road trip and my routine is messed up. But whether it's one or seven serenades, the first threshold is location. A bunch of people on the list are in Europe and Asia, so I've got to keep the day and time in mind. For friends in Hong Kong or Beijing, I usually whistle the day before their birthday (according to eastern time in the U.S.); the twelve-hour time difference can be a deal breaker if I wait until ten in the morning my time, because it's ten in the evening their time on their birthday. This way, I can get them in their morning and kick-start the day with a happy tune.

Then there's the serenade hierarchy. It's always preferable whistling in person, but that usually only works for colleagues, immediate family, and birthday parties. If that's not possible, I go for a live phone call or leave a voicemail. As a last resort, I record a serenade on my iPhone and text or e-mail it to the birthday boy or girl. This last option, more and more, has become the default, because getting anybody live on the phone these days is difficult, and bizarrely, many voicemails think I'm a fax machine and won't let me leave a message. Every time I get someone's voicemail, I pray that I can make it through the entire song before getting cut off.

But real time is best, whether in person or on the phone. There's nothing like the immediacy of a live audience to bring out the best my lips have to offer. At work, I am routinely summoned to conference rooms around the DC office to deliver a whistle before the cupcakes are consumed. It's always a lot of fun. I try to make each serenade special. At one point, I was doing so many birthday whistles in group settings with many of the same people in the room that I developed different versions.

There's the standard version, which is regal in feel, with a trumpet voluntary-like intro; a '50s-rock rendition; a heavy metal/ACDC-like version where I channel Brian Johnson's scratchy voice and Angus Young's gyrating guitar; and the reggae version, which works well in groups of three to five people. For larger groups, the version has to be bold and upbeat; a more deliberate and delicate reggae version would fall flat. My plan is to develop a few more, so I have a stable of versions that birthday boys and girls can choose from. This approach also helps when people save versions on their voicemail year after year.

Live performances on the phone work a lot better than one might think. My theory is that people care little for fidelity, and focus on the oddity and intent instead. It's sort of like beer at a keg party in college—whoever asked what kind of beer it was? That was missing the point; it was beer.

"Hold on, let me put you on speakerphone." I've heard this countless times from people I've caught in the middle of a birthday dinner or party. They shush whatever hubbub surrounds them, and then I hear: "Okay, we're ready."

I then launch into as rousing a version of "Happy Birthday" as I can muster. I rarely know who or how many are on the other end of the phone, but once someone opts for the group serenade, it's all about a muscular performance.

Two times, good buddies had me call into large parties they were hosting for family members. One was on Cape Cod, MA, in a barn that had been converted into a party hall. Harry had me call at a precise moment, silenced the crowd of several dozen, held his cell phone aloft, and let me loose. The roar of the crowd was wild and delightfully satisfying, despite the weird disembodied feeling of it all. One minute there was tons of hubbub, the next there was silence, with all eyes fixed on the hoisted cellphone. Then there was some freaky dude whistling "Happy Birthday" for their dear friend Katie, and then it was back to partying.

The other time, it was a birthday party on the outskirts of London for a friend's sister. Despite it being across the pond, the reaction was identical. The whistle was a hit, fleeting and effervescent, like the bubbles in their champagne.

Whether I'm calling a barn on Cape Cod or a friend at home, I deliver most of the serenades from my office at work. My work neighbors have gotten used to the muffled sound of the birthday song from behind my closed door. Whenever I get a new office neighbor, I warn him or her about the whistle. They don't seem to mind, but you never know. I also whistle for people from my car on the way to work or on the way home. It helps me focus on positive things rather than nasty Washington, DC traffic.

Vacations, weekends, work trips, and forgetfulness force me to whistle from wherever I am. I've whistled from the bathroom of a taxiing jumbo jet, lodges in remote Colorado and South Dakota, many an airport (replete with muffled gate announcements in the background), rest stops on fifty-mile bike rides, and my bed at ten at night, having realized soon before hitting the hay that a few birthdays had almost slipped away. In those cases, I usually send a recorded version, not wanting to disturb people late at night.

Sometimes I wonder how sustainable this model is. Committing to whistle for hundreds of people indefinitely occasionally freaks me out. What if I grow tired of it, or just don't feel like it anymore? Can I let all those people down? (Would they even notice?) It feels like my wife and I have had a fourth child, a responsibility we can never shirk. As with any child, there are joys and struggles, but the net is overwhelming positive—and the birthday serenades are a lot cheaper than kids!

Just as my wife and I can't remember what it was like before we had kids, after more than twenty years and more than 5,000 birthday serenades, I remember no before and imagine no after. The die is cast. This is what I do; I love it, and I am blessed by it.

"How do people get on the list?" I am sometimes asked. Admittedly, it's more circumstance than science. On one hand, there are the obvious ones: family and close friends. Then their children sometimes get added. Lots of colleagues are on the list. A bunch of moms and dads of friends have been added over the years.

I love it when people demand to be put on the birthday list. These are birthday aficionados who know what they want and see the power of the whistle. Such folks revel in their special day without embarrassment.

Depending on the year, around five to ten percent of the people on the list are complete strangers. In recent years, I've donated packages of ten birthday whistles to charity auctions. Soon after an auction, I get a somewhat sheepish call from the winner, wondering what she got herself into. It's pretty simple, I say. Give me the names, phone numbers, time zone, D.O.B., and any special instructions for ten of your family and friends, and I'll call them on their birthdays...anywhere in the world.

I get some of the most unusual reactions upon calling those people. When I ask if this is the birthday boy or girl, my query is usually met with suspicion. "Who is this?" they demand. "Sure, this is Chris Ullman, four-time international whistling champion, calling to wish you a "Happy Birthday" on behalf of so and so." The reactions run the gamut from "Oh," and "Okay," to "Awesome," and "Wow." There's rarely a conversation after I deliver the whistle. They are typically in shock, and just say thanks and goodbye.

Birthday shock and awe...mission accomplished!

In June of 2016, I did a radio interview on whistling. The host asked me why I whistle for people on their birthdays, and out popped a description I had never used before. I called it a "ministry." The word startled me as it left my lips. *A ministry?* Even the radio host was a bit perplexed, asking what I meant by that.

I silently pondered. *I'm a corporate communications executive who whistles for people on their birthdays. That's a hobby. A fun pastime. This is not rocket science or spiritual counseling. I'm not a minister or a priest or someone who's taken a vow of poverty in service to a flock. A ministry? Seems like a stretch.*

But the more I thought about it, it made perfect sense. My whistle is a tool, a means to touch people's hearts and lives in simple ways that deliver joy and goodwill. It's not about God, necessarily, the way a traditional ministry would be premised or motivated. That said, it is about the dignity and value of human life, and the joy and importance of service that my faith teaches.

Think about the people in your life. Their foibles and eccentricities notwithstanding, every one of them is special, with unique gifts that touch your life in some way, big or small. It's *that* that the whistle tries to acknowledge in a simple and enjoyable way.

Also, in a hyper-busy culture where every minute is accounted for, the whistle is a tiny respite, a whimsical relief valve. That's even true for bigwigs, the rich and powerful and well-credentialed, who are always being watched and judged, and for whom being simply human can seem like a weakness.

All the psycho-babble aside, the "Happy Birthday" whistle is sweet, pure fun, and there's always need for more good, clean, joyous fun in this world.

CHAPTER 6
Do You Have a Real Job?

"YOU SHOULD JOIN THE CHOIR."

"I want to *whistle* with the choir."

"You should join the choir and sing."

"No…oh…oh…a-ha…okay. Got it."

Another non-believer…how ironic.

I joined Blessed Sacrament Catholic Church in Alexandria, Virginia in 1997, and was soon impressed with the quality of the music program.

After Mass one Sunday, I cornered the director. "Hi. My name is Chris Ullman and I'm a new parishioner here, and I have this unusual hobby. I'm a champion whistler. I enjoy the choir, and would like to know if you're open to having me perform with your group sometime."

The smack-down was swift and bloodless. So much so, I initially presumed he didn't understand the question—but it was me who didn't understand the response, hence my asking a second time.

Some people get it; some don't. There is little in between. Some see the potential, while others are repulsed by the prospect. It's like whistling itself, a genetic phenomenon: you either can or you can't.

Over the years, there have been many WWF-like smack-downs. Another that stands out took place at a high school carwash fundraiser in the summer of 2012.

Driving along West Braddock Road in Alexandria, Virginia, a few blocks from my house one Saturday afternoon, came the frantic invitation of high school students seeking customers. Kids pointing and beckoning and jumping and waving, taking their marketing jobs seriously. In a split second, I spotted dirt on the hood of the car, felt like doing something nice, and joined the carwash queue.

"How much?"

"Just a good will donation."

"What's the cause?"

"T.C. Williams High School Orchestra."

Exiting my car, I bee-lined over to the most adult-looking person to learn more.

The conductor was a young woman in her late twenties to early thirties. I introduced myself and asked a few questions about her orchestra. The car was now being rinsed, so my window of opportunity was closing. No time for a long introduction. In a frontal assault, I told her of my whistling credentials and asked if she'd be interested in me performing with her orchestra sometime. Of course, I referenced having performed with the National Symphony Orchestra and a bunch of others. I tried to sound matter of fact and imply that performing with her orchestra was the next logical step.

I might as well have said I play the kazoo, her reaction was so milquetoast. She took my business card, making no commitments. The drying was done and my car was ready. They did a nice job. I never heard from her.

Then again, I could have followed up and pursued her, but that's not my style. Whether it's ego or a fierce sense of propriety, I don't beg. Even when dating, I was pretty utilitarian. My typical invitation consisted of two parts: "Are you *interested* and *available* to do X, Y, or Z?" After two declines, I moved on.

I've never been one to badger people, because I don't like to be badgered. I just treat people like adults and hope they act like it.

There is another school of thought. One time, I asked David Rubenstein, one of the greatest fundraisers of all time, the key to raising capital and getting people to do what you want them to do. He said that you have to be relentless. Never accept no—badger people…in a nice, respectful way.

Hhhmmm. Maybe that's why he's a billionaire and I'm not.

At this point in my life, I'm so busy with the day job and family that I don't have the time or interest to do heavy marketing. I rely on serendipity, chance encounters that yield whistling fruit.

Why did the two conductors shun my whistling? Who knows? Maybe they think it's weird, unserious, or kitschy. I suspect it's a combination of personal preference and where they fall on the innovation spectrum. Some people's life perspectives are more open to change and different ways of thinking than others. Maybe these people could be won-over if I adopted the Rubenstein method of persistence.

In the end, it's probably two parts numbers and one part persuasion. The more people I encounter, the more believers I will find, some of whom may need a little nudging to win them over.

Regardless of how open or closed someone is to new things, there's also a systemic roadblock that makes it harder to embrace serious whistling. It's a legitimacy gap. What makes something legitimate, serious art? What makes something corny, funny novelty? That's the great existential question among serious whistlers. In my experience, most people consider whistling novelty and not art—why?

I have long-believed that it's a vicious cycle. Because there is hardly any music written for lip, it lacks the validation that comes from talented composers writing music for an instrument and accomplished musicians bringing it to life.

Right now, try to think of songs that feature whistling; you can probably only come up with a handful. You might be thinking of the introduction to Billy Joel's *The Stranger*, and then there's the whistle riff in "The Dock of the Bay" by Otis Redding. If you're a senior, then you surely remember that Bing Crosby's crooning was sometimes accompanied by his whistling. There are a handful of whistling tunes in

Disney classics. Don't forget Sergio Leone's spaghetti westerns *A Fistful of Dollars, For a Few Dollars More,* and *The Good, The Bad and The Ugly.* Each features whistling in their theme songs, care of composer Ennio Morricone. For Broadway enthusiasts, how about "I Whistle a Happy Tune" from the musical *The King and I*? I saw it on Broadway when I was fifteen years old, and was excited to hear whistling in such a fancy setting. There's even whistling in Johann Strauss's opera *Die Fledermaus.* (One time I coached a talented tenor who needed help with the whistling part for a college production of the piece.)

My favorite is the marching prisoners of war in the 1957 film *The Bridge on the River Kwai* knocking out a rousing version of the "Colonel Bogey March." Whistling was a way to maintain dignity and order in the midst of brutality, chaos, and death. Thankfully, I've never had to use my whistle to help me manage mayhem.

Perhaps the most famous whistling song ever is the theme song to *The Andy Griffith Show.* Over the years, I've been asked to whistle "The Fishin' Hole" countless times. I always oblige, though I secretly wish the person were asking for a Beethoven symphony.

A musicologist could compile an exhaustive list of songs that feature whistling, but it would be depressingly short—maybe forty to fifty songs from modern musical history.

Perhaps a more likely reason that whistling elicits such stark reactions is that many people find it annoying. Heck, under certain circumstances, whistling even drives me nuts. When I worked at the U.S. Securities and Exchange Commission, I had to quell an uprising on my team caused by a colleague who whistled incessantly around the office. Several people, who couldn't take it anymore, approached me and demanded action. I called the puckered offender into my office and said he needed to put the kibosh on the whistling.

He was startled. A quick wit, he asked if I saw the irony. Of course, I said, but peace in the office trumps habitual whistling. I said I would have been more on his side if he had a larger repertoire (he usually whistled one song over and over), but it was too late at this point; the troops were restless and demanded his lips!

Since most people can whistle, but not well, it is consigned to the bottom shelf in the music department, just above kazoos. Talk about irony. In this case, whistling's simplicity and commonplace nature doesn't gain adherents and credibility and momentum; rather it diminishes and undermines. How could something that simple and prevalent be serious or enjoyable?

Since most people haven't heard an accomplished whistler, they don't know what they're missing. They're stuck in the "Uncle Fred" time warp, where, growing up, he was the only person they heard whistle a lot. Dear Uncle Fred was not that good, and his breath was nasty too. What happens when people hear accomplished whistling for the first time? Most people are amazed. There's wonder and delight in their voices. They ask questions—lots of them. "How long have you been doing this? How did you get started? Do you practice?" This is most common in adults, who think they've seen and heard it all. It's like finding out you've been singing the wrong words in your favorite song for twenty-five years—startling, but exciting.

So, is there hope to win over the masses?

Absolutely.

It will require a unique set of circumstances, the right person and the right song at the right moment. We whistlers have the ball on our own one-yard line, with the expanse of ninety-nine yards before our lips and lots of minutes on the clock. It can happen, but the odds are daunting. So we try harder, and learn from the past.

Interest in whistling has ebbed and flowed through the decades in the U.S. One of my whistling buddies, Steve Herbst, even has a motto: "Whistling is an idea whose time has returned!" That pre-supposes that it was once here. Though I haven't asked him, I suspect he'd agree with me that his motto is mostly aspirational, not today's reality. It's like that old riddle, what's always coming but never arrives? Answer: tomorrow.

But does that stop us serious whistlers? Heck no. We lather our lips with ChapStick, pucker, and blow.

I am an eternal optimist, so I know this journey is worthy and filled with hope. How do I know? I have definitive proof.

Putting reluctant conductors to shame are the many brides who have asked me to whistle at their weddings, both the ceremony and reception. Now, that is courage in the face of tradition.

In 1997, my friend Elizabeth Friedel asked me to whistle at her wedding. I was single at the time and had never been involved with the planning of a wedding, but I had been to enough of them to know they are complicated affairs that require military precision and skills on par with nuclear arms treaty negotiators.

I wasn't privy to the negotiations with her fiancé and mom, but I did know this amazing woman had bicycled across the United States a year before, so she was strong, determined, and fierce in the face of adversity.

As for the role Elizabeth wanted me to play, it was integral. She was all-in with the whistling. My job was to whistle three pieces during the service: Pachelbel's Canon in D for the processional; Schubert's Ave Maria mid-way through; and Purcell's Trumpet Tune in D for the recessional. The first and last were with organ accompaniment, while piano joined me in the honoring of Christ's mother.

It ended up being an amazing experience, though I was terrified going in. Elizabeth had more confidence in me than I had in myself. Run-throughs with my accompanist went well, which helped me relax and, most importantly, reminded me that this wasn't a concert; my job was to help create a lovely environment for the bride and groom and their friends and family.

As guests watched the beautiful bride gracefully processing, I was focused on the score, though I did see a couple of faces glance in my direction, probably wondering what that funky sound was. On the other hand, some guests were shocked to hear the music was whistled, presuming it was a flute at work.

Each of the pieces went well from my perspective, though the final and most important verdicts were rendered by the bride and her mom at the reception. Elizabeth was delighted and her mom was happy. Mission accomplished.

My job over, I settled into the wedding reception, hoping to have a fun and relaxing evening. Toward the end of the party, I had a fleeting chance encounter with the world's richest man.

Microsoft founder Bill Gates, a friend of the groom, was at the wedding and reception. As he was leaving the event, Elizabeth's new husband Jonathan introduced me to him. He realized I was the whistler from the ceremony, and casually asked, "Do you have a real job?" I suspect the notion of someone able to sustain himself as a whistler did not compute in his logical brain.

"Yes," I assured him, I had a real job, and it wasn't whistling. He seemed relieved.

I got a kick out of the whole thing. Doing something that got the world's richest man to pause and think was pretty cool. His reaction, though shows how much work there is to do to educate and win people over. A handful of accomplished whistlers and I are trying to change that reality, two ears at a time.

My big chance came a few years later.

Sitting in my office at Carlyle, the phone rang; it was a talent scout from Cirque du Soleil. I could hardly believe my ears: would I like to join the circus? They were auditioning for a lead role in *Corteo*, a production featuring a whistler.

What little kid hasn't thought of running away and joining the circus? What stressed out, overworked, sleep-deprived parent hasn't thought the same? A life of freedom and adventure, a new city every day, strong, bendable and lithe people—finally, my chance had come.

Join the circus...hhhmmm? *Of course, when can I start?*

Wait...what about the wife, kids, job, and mortgage?

Oh, to be twenty-three again and not have any obligations to humans or banks, to do and go as one pleases. Nonetheless, I seriously entertained the prospect of giving up my challenging and lucrative job, casting aside my family, and abandoning my mortgage. That lasted about five minutes. The fantasy of living as an itinerant whistler as part of the world's premier circus was fun while it lasted. (As I declined the opportunity, I recommended a fine whistler, Robert Stemmons, who got the job and toured the world with *Corteo*. He loved the experience.)

I wonder how Bill Gates would have responded if I'd said, "Yes, I whistle in the circus."

A *Whistle* That Touches My Heart

Name: John Heine
Home: Springfield, VA
Job: Retired communications professional
John's *Whistle*: The best carrot cake in the world
How I Know John: From 1997 to 2001, I was the head of public affairs at the U.S. Securities and Exchange Commission. John Heine was my deputy.

***Whistle* in Action**: John Heine's carrot cake is famous. During the four years John and I worked together at the U.S. Securities and Exchange Commission, he made carrot cakes to celebrate the birthdays of each member of our eight-person public affairs team. In the sixteen years since I left the Commission, John has made a cake for me pretty much every year. I don't even have to ask, he just volunteers. Beneath thick cream cheese frosting speckled with diced pecans resides layer upon layer of moist cake riddled with cinnamon and shaved carrot. It tastes great, and is the best-smelling cake I've ever had. So much so that during those years at the SEC when I was on a diet, I still claimed my slice of cake at staff birthday parties and inhaled deep breaths of its exquisite bouquet throughout the day (somewhat odd, but totally defensible!). John was a securities law and regulation guru, but his cakes may be his true legacy. The other day, I ran into a reporter who used to cover the SEC, and she asked if John was still making his carrot cake. "He is," I said, "and I am the blessed beneficiary of his simple culinary gift."

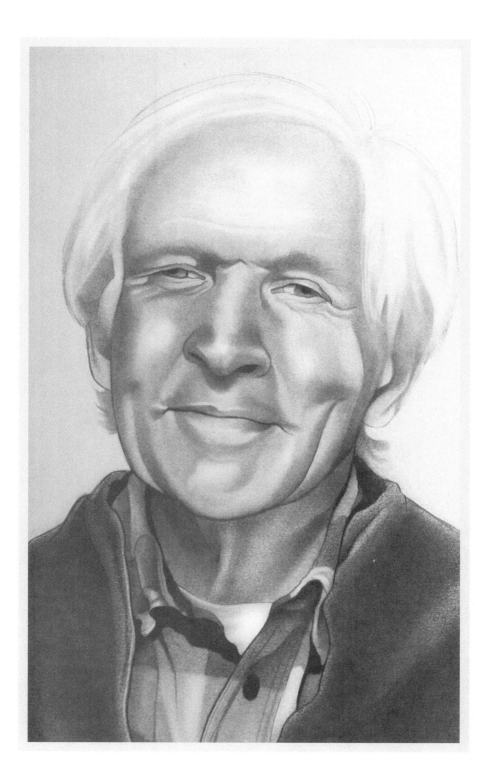

CHAPTER 7
Happy Birthday, Becky

THE PLANE HAD JUST LEFT THE GATE, rumbling toward the runway, Turkish Air headed from Istanbul to Hong Kong. My body was still adjusting to the radical time change, so I was eager to close my eyes for a few hours.

My cell phone vibrated. It was my wife Kristen, asking if I had whistled for Becky's birthday. Becky is our babysitter Rocky's mother.

"Ahhhgggh, we're about to take off!"

"Well, if you like date night, you better whistle for her."

I scanned the business class cabin and saw no flight attendants about; even they were buckled in.

The restroom was ten feet away. I unbuckled and was inside the bathroom in seconds. Speed-dial got me to the U.S. quickly, and thankfully Becky's voicemail picked up; no time for chitchat.

I delivered a swift and lively "Happy Birthday," flushed for effect, and made it back to my seat as the nose wheels left the ground.

Tragedy narrowly averted. Date night lives on!

CHAPTER 8
The Lone Ranger Is in the Mood

"I HATE TO PUT YOU ON THE SPOT, but could you whistle something for us?"

"Hey, everyone, be quiet. My friend Chris is a champion whistler and he's going to do a song for us."

"WHISTLE!!"

Whether it was a sheepish request or a demand, virtually every party I went to for a fifteen year stretch, starting with my first victory at the whistling competition in 1994, involved some on-the-spot whistling. It didn't matter if it was an intimate dinner party, cocktail reception, wingding kegger, or wedding, inevitably someone would put the squeeze on me (not that it required a lot of arm-twisting!) to whistle.

Typically it was just the people in my immediate vicinity who were commanded to stop what they were doing and pay attention to the whistler. Sometimes, quite awkwardly, the whole party would come to a grinding halt as the host or a somewhat inebriated person turned the music off and, like a carnival barker, got everyone's attention focused on me; I became the performer at the center of the three-ring circus.

I quickly figured out that having a few songs ready to go was important so that I didn't futz around trying to come up with the "right" song once the spotlight was pointed at me. Two songs became my go-to command performance pieces: "In the Mood" by Glenn Miller and the finale of the *William Tell Overture* by Gioachino Rossini.

The first piece was a hugely popular big band swing song from 1940. It was on an album my parents had when I was growing up called *The Glenn Miller Story*—and what a story it was. Miller was a great trombonist turned conductor, who enlisted in the military and traveled the world entertaining Allied forces until dying in a plane crash over the English Channel. I whistled the tune a lot on my paper route from thirteen to sixteen years old, and then in college I became a fan of jazz trumpeter Jeff Tyzik, who did a totally rocking version of the song. It was his arrangement of "In the Mood" that I whistled all those years.

The *William Tell Overture* came into my repertoire also during the paper route era (1976-1979) through the *120 Music Masterpieces* collection. *William Tell* was Italian composer Rossini's thirty-ninth and final opera. The finale of the overture, known as "March of the Swiss Soldiers," is the section and tune that most people are familiar with. The song is generally known by another name—*The Lone Ranger* song, because it was the theme song to a popular TV show of the same name that aired from 1949 to 1957. *The Lone Ranger* was about a former Texas Ranger who teamed with a Native American to fight outlaws in the wild American West.

A song about getting ready for some loving, and a song about guns and fighting injustice—the juxtaposition never occurred to me until years later. Regardless of the purported meaning of the song, the tunes were catchy and the rhythms were complex. Audiences always reacted well to them.

Washington, DC is a company town, and the product is politics. No widgets are made here. We're all about words—written and spoken—with lots of regulations, laws, taxes, and spending thrown in. The city of Washington is segregated by both race and party. Just as people tend to live with people of the same race, they tend to be friends with people of the same party or ideology. That's unfortunate.

I'm a conservative, but have many friends who are hard-core liberals. I love it. We never run out of things to talk and argue about. On a recent bike ride, my friend Michael Abrams and I debated and argued about public policy for four straight hours while cycling along at sixteen miles per hour. We hadn't seen each other in a while, so we had a lot of arguing to catch up on. With the 2016 presidential race well under way, there was a lot of fresh material to discuss.

From 1994 to 2001, I was single and willing to travel, so I went to a lot of parties in DC and NY, my current and former homes. When asked to whistle, sometimes I'd just launch into a song, and other times I'd ask people what they wanted to hear. One time I was at my dear friend Sofia's apartment in New York City at her annual birthday party when the demand for a whistle arose. I asked the collected guests if they wanted to hear *The Lone Ranger* song or "In the Mood." By enthusiastic acclamation, they chose the latter. (I also whistled "Happy Birthday.")

At many parties in DC, the same experience played out over and over. I won four championships during that period, so requests to whistle were frequent. At more than a few of those parties, when given a choice, most audiences usually went with *The Lone Ranger* song. Happy to oblige, I gave the people what they wanted.

Then one day it dawned on me. In DC, most of my friends were conservatives, while in NY, most of my friends were liberals. When there was ideological homogeneity and a choice, the liberals went with the feel good song and the conservatives went with the guns and law song. Mind you, this was not a scientific study, but the patterns were stark and consistent over time.

As for me, I'm an ecumenical kind of guy, so I like all kinds of music, have all kinds of friends, and think that love and guns are completely compatible, though holsters are known to chaff bare skin.

Now that I know these songs are a barometer for political ideology, I will occasionally put them to the test to see how homogeneous the audience is. It's a little sly, but if the verdict is clear, I will reveal what I did, to the delight of the audience, for whom the news is just an affirmation of what they already knew. Birds of a feather flock together.

CHAPTER 9
Happy Birthday, Joannie

SMILING IS AN OCCUPATIONAL HAZARD for a whistler. They're like oil and water. It's one or the other, as a smiling face couldn't form a pucker in a million years. One pulls the lips apart and the other draws them together.

But smiling, like yawning, is contagious. So, as more and more small group settings have required my puckered prowess, I've had to develop my game face, a mental state that allows me to block out distractions as I whistle a happy tune. It took years, but now when someone is smiling or giggling, even just a few feet away, or on the phone in my ear, I can maintain my pucker.

And then I was tested.

I met Debby Kelly at her son Jason's book launch party. He had just published his first book, a primer on the private equity industry featuring my employer, The Carlyle Group. Debby and I hit it off right away. She's friendly and sassy with a playful Atlanta-derived accent. As the party was winding down, I found myself hanging with Jason and his parents and a couple of other guests in the living room of his parents' home in leafy Northwest DC.

In a "guess what freaky thing my friend Chris is good at" moment, the conversation turned to whistling, care of Jason, which led to some storytelling and a demonstration. I told how I whistle "Happy Birthday" for people, including Jason, and that's when Debby asked how she could get on the list. Out came my iPhone calendar, and thus a new friendship was born.

Six months went by, and on March 24, I called Debby and serenaded her. Within a year, most of her family was on the list. They crept on person by person, via e-mails from Debby asking me to help celebrate the birth of this or that loved one.

The ultimate test was Debby's sister Joannie. I called her cold on August 16.

"Hi, is this the birthday girl?"

"Why, yeahs, it is. Whooo's theis?" she drawled like her sweet sister Debby.

"This is Chris Ullman, and I'm the four-time international whistling champion, calling to serenade you on your special day on behalf of your sister Debby."

"Oh, myyy!"

"Are you ready?"

"Yeahs, I ahhm."

Contemporaneous with the first note of the fanfare introduction, the laughing began.

It was hearty, full-throated, natural. The actual whistle, or the act of being serenaded, tickled her in some way and triggered a fusillade of uncontrollable joy. It was quite impressive.

I was startled at first, and came within a micrometer of joining in her hilarity. But my game face withstood the blast of laughter and I soldiered on, focused on my task.

Soon enough, we both stopped what we were doing and started talking. Joannie was grateful and a bit embarrassed. I was amazed I'd made it through the song. We hit it off, just as her sister and I had.

A year later, I serenaded her again. I braced for the laugh, but none came. Like a crush that settles into love, the whistle no longer startled her, but it seemed to please her just the same.

CHAPTER 10

Oh Say Can You Whistle

AT THE TAP ON MY SHOULDER, I turned around; a lovely woman in her mid-twenties was standing there.

"Mr. Ullman?"

"Yes."

"Sorry to interrupt. Mr. Castellini would like to see you," she said while motioning to a table a few over from mine.

"Okay," I said, wondering who Mr. Castellini was.

I walked the thirty or so feet to his table, and by process of elimination, figured out which one was Bob Castellini. It helped that I knew the other three people at his table. One was my boss, Dan D'Aniello, chairman of The Carlyle Group; the second was former vice presidential candidate and then-Ways & Means Chairman Paul Ryan (now Speaker of the U.S. House of Representatives); and beside Paul was his wife Janna.

Bob rose and greeted me, introducing himself as the owner of the Cincinnati Reds baseball team. Not being a big sports fan, he could have told he owned the New York Giants and I would have believed him.

Perhaps not wanting his coffee to get cold, he got right to the point.

"I hear you're a pretty good whistler. Can I hear some?"

"What would you like to hear?

"Well, the national anthem, of course."

"The whole thing? Right here?"

He just looked at me.

Scanning the rest of the table, I saw big smiles on their faces. At a minimum, they thought the exchange, including my evident surprise, was pretty funny.

I thought for a moment, whipping through the words to find a good place to start.

"The Star Spangled Banner" has an A-A-B-C structure, which means that the first two verses have the same notes, then there's a short bridge to the march-like finale.

"Okay, I'll do the finale."

Notes came out of my lips corresponding to, "Oh, say does that star-bangled banner yet wave o'er the land of the free and the home of the brave?" I dragged out "wave" with a warble, and went up an octave on "free," ending with a soft trill on "brave." Though only a snippet, it's the most dramatic part of the song and allows the most creativity.

The four of them burst into applause.

"Okay. You're in."

"In what?"

"I'd like you to whistle the national anthem at a Reds game."

"Wow, that would be great," I said, with a sense of the wonder at the unexpected pitches life throws.

If I had actively sought the opportunity to whistle at a Reds game, it probably would have taken years of effort, travel, and persistence, with a low probability of success. Here it came out of left field, and took a minute or so. I didn't even have time to get nervous.

Bob sat down as I went around the table and said hi to Dan, Paul, and Janna. Paul leaned in and said I should thank Janna for turning Bob onto my whistling and putting the squeeze on him to have me perform at his stadium.

Ah, the fruits of chance meetings.

Earlier in the day, I was hanging out in the lobby of the resort and conference center where the American Enterprise Institute, a think tank based in Washington, DC, was having its annual gab-fest, a gathering of smart and powerful political and business types who advocate for limited, effective government. Dan D'Aniello, who is also vice chairman of AEI, invited me to the event. If you like policy and politics, it's a great place to see, hear, and chat with conservative policy thinkers and bigwig politicians.

That's how I'd come to run into Paul and Janna Ryan in the lobby. Back in 1995 to 1996, Paul and I had worked together on Capitol Hill on the House Budget Committee. I was the Committee spokesman, and he was a budget analyst working for a Committee member.

I had heard Paul was going to speak at the AEI conference, and was hoping to say hi if I had the chance. Well, there I was people-watching when he walked up, said hello, and introduced me to his wife Janna.

Paul instantly launched into an excited description of my whistling to his bride. What I've found over the years is that most politicians (the good ones, at least), latch onto some trait or accomplishment or memory about the countless people they meet so they can have something to talk about when they encounter them and have to introduce them to other people. While I am proud of my whistling accomplishments, I sometimes wish someone like Paul would introduce me as "one of the best PR people in DC."

As one of my Carlyle colleagues once said to me, "Unless you cure cancer someday, you'll always be known as the whistler." Since there's no chance of me curing cancer (chemistry was never my thing), and whistling is more intriguing to people than PR, I think my colleague is right. I don't lose sleep over this, and talking about whistling is always fun. It also leads to opportunities to do the national anthem at major league sporting events.

The first time I whistled the national anthem at a baseball game was in the early 1990s, at a Bowie Baysox game. Like so many of the whistling gigs and things I've done over the years, that gig came about following an idea that just popped into my head. One day I thought, *wouldn't it be cool to whistle the national anthem at a baseball game?* So, keeping in line with my management philosophy of embracing incrementalism, I targeted a local minor league team rather than jumping right into the majors.

I cold-called the Baysox, a Double-A team based in Bowie, MD, a suburb of Washington. The marketing person I talked to was open to the idea of me whistling the anthem. He asked for a demo tape and some other proof of concept, such as news articles, to prove that I was the real deal and not some convincing freak. (He didn't phrase it like that, but I'm sure that's what he was thinking.) To my delight, he liked what he heard, and invited me to perform the national anthem later that season.

That first national anthem pales in comparison to the version I do today. My rendition was perfectly acceptable. I'd call it a "straight" version, meaning it had no whirly-gigs (trills or warbles), octave jumps, or tempo changes. Though I've known the song my whole life, at that point, I hadn't made it my own. For my inaugural performance, I was shooting for strong, not innovative or great. No need for a homer when a double would do.

The audience enjoyed, the skeptical marketing guy was pleased, and my family was excited to see it live. More importantly, that good experience set me on a course to find and do more national anthems.

In the late '90s, I got my big break. My then-girlfriend's father, Ray, was friends with the management of the Charlotte Hornets NBA basketball team. Ray made the pitch, and they thought it was worthy. Ray must have been hopeful that we'd get married; otherwise, he might not have gone out on such a limb to get me the gig. Well, he called it; his daughter Kristen and I were married in 2001.

I went into rehearsal mode, whistling my usual Strauss waltzes and the national anthem at a feverish pace. The more I whistled "The Star Spangled Banner", the better I understood it. Note by note and section by section, I made it my own. The neat thing is that my arrangement of it continues to evolve. The way I perform it today is different from that first NBA game, which was more advanced than the first time with the Baysox.

Leading up to the game, I was worried that the audience wouldn't like having a whistler perform the anthem. Even though it was more than seven years in the rear mirror, Roseanne Barr's ghastly (and brutally attacked) rendition of the national anthem at a San Diego Padres game in 1990 still stuck in people's heads. Of course, I was planning on a pitch-perfect, respectful version, with no crotch-grabbing or spitting—but still, a whistler?

I arrived at the stadium on the big day and stepped onto the pregame conveyor belt. Two hours before jump ball, I rehearsed at center court. The stadium was empty, which felt weird, like seeing a favorite actor without make-up in sweatpants walking the dog on a Saturday morning on the streets of Chelsea in lower Manhattan. I had never been in such a large arena when it was empty. It was so quiet and sterile, a reminder that the vessel is not as important as the contents that are poured into it.

My sound check went well. To go from whistling around the house and in the car to the big, deep, echoing sound of an arena made me feel much bigger physically, like I was the Wizard behind Oz's curtain. This gave me much needed confidence and peace. Now all I had to do was stay calm for another ninety minutes, hoping my mouth would stay moist and my lips limber.

Like a forest coming to life as the sun starts to rise, little by little, lots of people came and went, each adding a piece to the game-day puzzle. A maintenance man wiped down the court, a junior staffer brought out towels, and then racks filled with dozens of balls were rolled in. Coaches and players arrived in ones and twos, the latter wearing sweats nearly as long as I was tall. Fans dribbled in, the VIPs among them getting photos with players. Bright digital ads came to life along LED screens that ringed the arena. The announcer did a sound check.

With minutes to go, I tried to keep my mind off the anthem by watching the players warm up and chatting with the staffer who shepherded me through the whole production. She told me exactly what was going to happen. First, the warming-up players, dozens of balls, and media doing pre-game interviews would leave the court; then the color guard would enter to the booming welcome of the announcer; then, on her cue, I would walk to the microphone at center court as the lights dimmed and the announcer introduced me.

She was right. With religious ritual and military precision, it all unfolded perfectly; major league sporting events are well-oiled machines.

"Ladies and gentlemen, please rise for our national anthem, which will be performed by Chris Ullman, the two-time international whistling champion."

I could picture lots of people who were barely paying attention turn to the person next to them and ask, "Did he say *whistler*?"

A rumble of discontent rippled through the crowd of 20,000…the ghost of Roseanne was clanging her chains. But the freight train was picking up speed, so there was no turning back.

I lifted the pitch pipe to my lips to ensure I started on the right note, therefore able to hit the high note at the end. (That was one of Roseanne's mistakes; without perfect pitch and no pitch pipe, she was doomed from the start. Grabbing her crotch and spitting at the end just sealed her fate.)

As the first notes filled the stadium, some fans started to whistle along with me while others continued talking. Perhaps they were expressing their displeasure with the unusual instrument performing our nation's sacred anthem.

As I worked my way through the first two verses that precede the lighter, delicate verse ("…and the rockets' red glare, the bombs bursting in air…"), I realized how quiet it had become. It was odd to have that many people in one space and you could hear a pin drop.

At that point in my national anthem career, I was not able to multitask, meaning focus on the performance and enjoy it at the same time. (That has happened only a couple of times, especially when I performed it at a Washington Wizards NBA game in 2015.) I had only one thing on my mind: delivering a great anthem, note perfect and well interpreted.

The U.S. national anthem is a notoriously hard song to sing. The words are complicated and the range of the tune is rather wide. Neither is a problem for me, though, as my range exceeds three octaves, and whistlers need to know notes, not words!

I slowed the pace down for the dramatic finale, emphasizing each word in staccato fashion ("Oh...say...does...th-at...star...span...gled... ba...n-er...y-et...wa-ve"), then smoothing it out ("o'er the la-nd of the") before jumping up an octave on the latter half of "free," driving the audience nuts, before winding it up with a trill on "brave."

Whoops of appreciation greeted my last notes. I bowed, waved, and walked off the court. My handler had a big smile on her face. The whole time, she had probably been wondering who had decided this was a good idea. To my utter surprise and delight, high fives and atta-boys lined the path on the way to my seat. It was a comforting experience.

I'm often asked if I'm paid to whistle the national anthem. The answer is no. Even if someone offered, I would decline. Getting paid to whistle is fine by me, but not for the anthem. Anyhow, supply outstrips demand, so there's no need to entice people to perform the anthem through a paycheck.

Two years later, Ray secured another national anthem for me at a Hornets' game. Coincidentally, it was once again against the LA Lakers. Like the first time, it went well, but with less grumbling from the audience. Enough of them probably heard me the first time, so I was a proven act.

Those two national anthems whet my appetite (and whistle) for more big games, but life and circumstance (busy job, three kids) got the best of me; more than ten years passed before I performed it at more big sporting events.

That said, I performed the anthem a bunch of times during those years at smaller events of a public policy nature. This enabled me to experiment with different arrangements and to learn how to enjoy the experience. I've gotten a much better sense of how special the anthem is to people. It's such a unifying song, even if people can't always remember the words.

In 2014 and 2015, I did three national anthems at major league games that came about through Carlyle connections. One time, I was at a business conference with David Rubenstein. At a reception before David gave a speech, I found myself standing next to him and Mark Lerner, one of the owners of the Washington Nationals baseball team. Being a bit of a shameless self-promoter, in a break in the conversation, I asked David if it was okay to mention my whistling to Mark. David, who's always been a fan of my whistling, said to go for it.

Mark's reaction was positive but non-committal. He said he'd think about it, and we should get in touch to discuss further. The seed was planted, and it didn't take long for the idea to bloom.

After David's speech, he unexpectedly called me to the stage to whistle for the audience of several hundred business people. This is one of the many neat things about being a brilliant and highly sought-after billionaire businessman. You can give a speech about the global economy, and then decide on a whim to have your spokesman whistle a song. I wasn't fully warmed up, but at least I had whistled for half an hour in the car on the way to work that morning.

As I approached the stage, I pondered what piece to do. I had recently started performing "The Battle Hymn of the Republic," so that seemed as good as any piece under the circumstances. Everyone in the audience seemed to agree, as the reaction to my rendition of the battle hymn was swift and thunderous. Actually, I think they were in shock, swept up by the cognitive dissonance. People don't whistle at business functions in Washington—or anywhere.

Moments after I left the stage, the event ended, and I headed for the exit in the back of the room. Mark Lerner bee-lined over to me and placed his business card in my hand while expressing amazement at my command performance. As if his wide eyes, enthusiastic handshake, and elbow grab weren't enough, he asked me to give him a call so he could get me on the schedule to perform the anthem. My head was spinning as I walked out of the venue.

A few months later, I stood behind home plate as the Nationals and Reds warmed up. It's a humbling experience to be on the field of a large stadium. Baseball stadiums make basketball arenas seem like cottages. My senses were in overdrive. Sights and sounds seemed brighter and crisper. I was transported back to the floor of Zion National Park in Utah (I camped there in the early '90s), where the canyon walls towered over me and I felt tiny. At times like that, I'm reminded of how big the world is and that I'm one tiny piece of the global puzzle. They help keep life in perspective.

In peaceful obscurity, amidst the pre-game hubbub, I stood behind home plate in my beige khakis and red polo shirt, in honor of the red-themed Nationals. Kristen and our then-eleven year-old son Justus were with me, while several dozen friends and colleagues were in the stands waiting for the big moment.

Usually I know exactly what version of the anthem I am going to do before I step out onto the field or court, but this time, I had an alternative end up my sleeve that I was willing to use if I felt good about how things were going halfway through the piece. Earlier that day, a new ending popped into my head while I was rehearsing. I'd go up an octave at the very end, on "brave," rather than my more traditional, conservative, and safer ending.

I was feeling a bit frisky and adventurous. It reminded me of the choice a sports team with a lead makes as it nears the end of the game. Do you play to win? Or do you play to not lose? It's safer to sit on a lead rather than extend the lead, but while playing to not lose can yield victory, it can demoralize the players and send the signal to fans that the team is not trying its hardest. Performing is exhilarating, and pushing the envelope makes it even more so. As with most things in life, the key is to strike a balance between risk and reward. My whole life, I've had a bias toward more risk, because the lure of excitement or victory or wealth or affirmation is appealing. That plus the fear of failure push me hard to be prepared and to achieve.

For an hour or so before show time, I was in a room alone, warming up, thinking happy thoughts and muttering an occasional prayer, asking God to help me make good use of the simple gift he had given me. I was nervous and confident, probably in equal amounts. Over the years, I've found they generally don't cancel each other out, yielding mush. Rather, nerves help to heighten my senses, and confidence enables me to stand in front of people and think I have a right to be there. They are opposite sides of the same coin, a fascinating mix of feelings.

At the appointed time, I left my rehearsal cocoon and arrived behind home plate. Like the Hornets-Lakers games, there was lots of pre-game hubbub—junior staffers scurrying around, bigwig players strutting about and signing autographs between batted balls, journalists interviewing people, and VIPs visiting with players and management. Thirty minutes before the first pitch, a worker arrived with a stencil in the shape of the Nationals' fancy script W. He laid it down a few feet behind the plate and sprayed a pure white substance on the exposed dirt, yielding a crisp W nearly three feet across, contrasting nicely with the light brown dirt. The microphone, with a bright red wind screen, was placed directly behind it. That would be my means of delivering a gentle breeze of air loudly enough for tens of thousands of people to hear.

With Kristen and Justus by my side, idle conversation and eager gawking at the spectacle around us kept me nicely distracted from the impending moment of truth.

As the players lined up along the first and third base lines, hats across their hearts, I gazed deep into the outfield in search of the American flag. There it was, not far from the Jumbotron, which would soon feature a scary close-up of my puckered lips.

The announcer's soothing voice ricocheted across the stadium, gently commanding the audience to rise for the national anthem, which would be performed by a whistler. My handler nodded me in the direction of the spray-painted W, out came my pitch pipe, and following a deep breath and a quick look around the stadium, the object of my desires came to fruition. I resisted retreating into my own world, and managed to keep my eyes open for most of the performance. Sure enough, there I was on the giant video screen. Watching a twenty-five foot version of me whistle was a weird out-of-body experience. Was I whistling, or were the giant lips on the screen whistling?

Mid-way through, filled with awe and confidence, I called an audible and decided to go with my new alternative end. *Why not*, I thought, *wasn't it time to play to win?* After jumping up an octave on the second half of "free" right near the end, I knew I'd be able to belt out an even higher note on "brave."

It worked. The already-startled crowd reacted. Utterly exuberant, I pumped my fist in the air. My intense minute and a half was done, and so was I. I went to my seat, basked in the gracious praise of my friends and lots of strangers, and settled in for the game, which the Nationals won.

―――――――――

My boss, David Rubenstein, is known around the world for his philanthropy and giving back to organizations that have impacted his life. Coming out of high school, he received a full scholarship to Duke University. It set him on a remarkable life journey, including a four-year stint as senior aide to President Jimmy Carter and founding The Carlyle Group, an investment firm. When he turned fifty-four, he decided it was time to start giving his money away. Duke, among many others, was a primary beneficiary of his generosity. Soon he was named to the Duke Board, and then he became chairman.

In my role as head of communications at Carlyle, I got to know the head of communications at Duke, Michael Schoenfeld. A few years into David's chairmanship, Michael called out of the blue and offered me the plumiest of plum whistling assignments: performing the national anthem at a Duke men's basketball game at Cameron Indoor Stadium.

I accepted, we set a date, and then I informed David. I could see the gears turning in his head. He determined he was available, and then he declared it was time for a road trip—a road trip like none I had ever done, even including lots of crazy ones in college.

A month later, David gathered a bunch of Carlyle colleagues, including several Duke alums, a few kids, and my bride, and off we took in his private jet. A bus met us at the airport in Raleigh Durham and brought us to the famous Cameron Indoor Stadium, a remarkably small arena built in 1940—but 9,300 insane Duke fans can make even a small arena seem huge.

I was warned in advance to prepare for a raucous experience, maybe even unalloyed disrespect from a tradition-bound audience. Michael, the PR guy, said that I would be the first person to whistle at Cameron, and he couldn't predict the reaction.

The Carlyle contingent was seated in the front row, mid-court, behind the scorer and announcer's table. Cheek to jowl, we were crammed in. Ray and Dale Ardizzone, my wife's father and brother, respectively, drove up from Charlotte to join in the festivities.

A pre-game ritual resembling the Hornets and Nationals beckoned me from the stands to the court. For a few minutes I paced on the sidelines, waiting for my moment before the self-proclaimed greatest and rowdiest fans in the NCAA.

The reaction to my introduction was the first sign that this was going to go well. Whistles and cheers greeted me as I walked onto the floor. Facing the color guard, I took a deep breath as I surveyed the masses, stacked high and tight, nearly touching the rafters in the seventy-five year-old building.

Away from the microphone, I blew into my pitch pipe. The note was locked in my brain. Then there was silence. Nearly 10,000 previously screaming humans were now perfectly quiet, on their feet, hands on hearts, waiting for a dose of patriotism. And I was going to administer it.

Dressed in blue jeans and a tight check-pattern shirt with the cuffs rolled up, I delivered a confident anthem with some nice tempo changes, march-like rhythms, and sweet warbles. The stadium's silence was broken as I jumped up an octave on "free," and the place went wild on "brave." It was louder than the major league basketball and baseball games I had whistled at. I bowed and returned to my seat. Duke went on to crush Boston College in a very exciting game.

Back on the bus we got, and on the plane home we went.

It was a magical experience from start to finish. I am so blessed to have this amazing gift and to be able to share it with people, and to have friends and bosses who are so supportive.

––––––––––––––

There's nothing like performing the national anthem, especially a hard fought one, which brings us back to the Reds.

After I left the AEI conference, having been invited by Bob Castellini to perform at a Reds game, I contacted the team's PR people in Cincinnati.

Crickets. My phone calls and e-mails were ignored. I soon realized what seemed to be happening, and it was just reward for me.

PR people have a dark part of their job description that few of us talk about. It's called cleaning up for the boss. Over the years, I've had lots of bosses who don't like to say "no." When they're at a public function and someone walks up to them and asks them to do something, such as give a speech, do a media interview, or take a meeting, the boss usually says "Sure, give my PR person a call."

When the PR person gets the inevitable call, the answer is often, "I'm sorry, the boss isn't available."

That's what I think happened with the Reds. When the PR people got my message, they were shocked and dismayed that the boss would agree to such a thing. So they worked to kill it.

I quickly grew annoyed and was about to send them a nasty-gram, but I stepped back and asked myself a question: *what is my objective?* My answer was to whistle the national anthem at a Reds game. A nasty-gram was not going to help achieve that, so I decided to be like David

Rubenstein and be relentless, nice, and focused on the brass ring. Every few weeks, I sent a nice note asking how things were going and if we could get a date on the calendar.

Months later, the logjam broke. One of their PR people contacted me and said they were open to it, but there were few dates left. I said I'd make whatever they offered work. They said people usually only got to perform the anthem if they bought 400 tickets, so this was a great privilege. I agreed. They said they wouldn't pay my expenses. I said no problem. We got a date on the calendar, which happened to be a game against the Washington Nationals.

The Great American Ball Park is a magnificent place, huge, new, and brightly modern. Whistling in such a large stadium is challenging because I'm hearing two whistles, one coming out of my mouth, and the other coming over the giant loudspeakers a second later. I had been warned that the sound delay was particularly pronounced at this stadium, so during the pre-game rehearsal, I focused intently on the sound coming directly from my mouth, ignoring the echo.

The anthem went very well. The crowd was into it. Perhaps to their own shock, the PR people loved it.

———————

Now that I have several baseball and basketball games under my whistling belt, I'm in the market for an NFL or college football game and an NHL game. It's just a matter of time before I meet the right people and make the pitch.

Meanwhile, I'll revel in having had the great honor of sharing our national anthem with people in a fresh way that stretched the boundaries of familiarity while introducing people to the versatility and power of the whistle.

A *Whistle* That Touches My Heart

Name: Father John Adams
Home: Washington, DC
Job: Catholic priest; President of So Others Might Eat (SOME)
Fr. John's *Whistle*: Love
How I Know Fr. John: I met Fr. John in 2010 through Carlyle co-founder Bill Conway when he was in the process of making a large, personal gift to the organization to build affordable housing for homeless people in Washington, DC. I helped out with the public announcement of the gift.

***Whistle* in Action**: Love is the most powerful *whistle* a person can have. Based on that, Fr. John has the loudest *whistle* I've ever heard. He and his team have dedicated their lives to helping poor people have productive and meaningful lives. SOME provides a variety of services, including housing, clothes, food, showers, medical and dental treatment, addiction treatment, and job training. The first time I met Fr. John, I was struck by his humble demeanor. It was all about his clients, not him. I asked him for advice regarding homeless people asking for money. "Look them in the eye...ask how they are doing...suggest they come to SOME for help." It wasn't as scary as I feared. I printed business cards with SOME's address and a list of their services, and following Bill Conway's lead, I started giving out five dollar Starbuck's gift cards. *There but for the grace of God go I.* In his thirty-eight years of leading SOME, Fr. John has helped many people on the lowest rungs of the economic ladder while enlisting the support of those who've already ascended it. He is a great gift to the Washington, DC community, and his selfless love has touched my heart and helped me better live my Christian faith.

CHAPTER 11

Happy Birthday, Man Friend

"HELLO?"

"Hey, it's Chris Ullman. Happy birthday!"

"Thanks, nice of you to remember."

"You bet. Are you ready for a serenade?"

"Oh, that's not necessary."

"No problem, I'm happy to do it."

"No. I'm fine. It was nice of you to call."

"Are you sure?"

"Yes. Thanks for thinking of me."

Hard to believe, for me at least, that not everyone likes being serenaded on their birthday.

What's odd is that these same men (and it's always men) are fine being serenaded live in person. It's live on the phone they don't like. It's visceral. There's no pondering or confusion. "Are you ready for a serenade?" "No!" Pretty straight-forward.

The first time this happened, I was perplexed and a little hurt. By the third time, I sensed a pattern and knew there was something else going on. Best I can tell, it's not about liking the serenade or not; it's about comfort, or lack thereof.

My theory is that these men decline the phone serenade because it feels too intimate to have another man whistle for them on the phone. It's as if my lips, through the magic of modern crystal-clear telecommunications, are close to their ears, faces, and God forbid, their lips! Obviously there's no spit-swapping going on over the phone; it's a feeling, a proximity thing. This is psycho-babble at its best, but I can't think of another reason why they decline.

In each of the cases where men have declined a phone serenade, I've whistled for them in person on previous birthdays. In those cases, we were alone in their offices at work when I delivered the serenade. You'd think that would make them even more uncomfortable than a phone call. Maybe it was just harder to turn me down in person than on the phone. I'm tempted to ask to ask these gentlemen about why they declined a phone whistle, but that would probably just compound the discomfort. Instead, I record the serenade and e-mail or text it to them.

The take-away for me is that, when inserting myself into people's birthday orbit, I need to remember it's about them and not me. I'm just a happiness delivery device.

CHAPTER 12
The Titanic Sails Again

THE BLACKBERRY VIBRATED in my pocket. "Hey, it's Chris."

"Hey buddy, how's the party?"

"Fun, catching up with folks from all over. How are things with the delegation?"

"Great. Can you do me a favor and come over to the Chamber to-morrow morning and whistle for the head of the delegation?"

"Sure. I can do a few standards, maybe "Take the 'A' Train" or a show tune."

"No, I need you to do a particular song."

"Okay. What song?"

"The theme song to the movie *Titanic*."

"Huh? I don't know that song."

"Come on, you saw the film."

"Yeah, when it came out who knows how many years ago."

"Can't you learn it?"

"When? It's already 9:30 at night, and I did plan on sleeping a little tonight."

"You'll be fine. Be at the U.S. Chamber across from the White House at 9:30 in the morning."

"Okay. See you then." #@8!!(&!!!

My eyes darted back and forth between the car in front of me and Kate Winslet in the passenger seat beside me. Earnest-looking, mid-word, her image on the iPad screen kept freezing as I listened to Celine Dion crooning the theme song to *Titanic* from a video on YouTube as I raced home.

Many thoughts raced through my brain.

This is not going well.

Don't worry, she'll thaw.

I'm screwed!

Don't be a pessimist!

I shut my eyes for a moment as I sigh-grunted, "Uuuuugghhh."

Keep your eyes on the road! Death and whistling are generally incompatible.

Celine was suddenly singing again: "…far, wherever you are, I believe that the heart does go on, once more you open the…"

Then she was gone, replaced by a frozen (literally and figuratively) Leonardo DiCaprio.

It was 10:30 at night, and in eleven hours, I was going to serenade the president of the Bank of China. And I didn't know the song.

The house was dark and quiet when I got home; Kristen and the kids were asleep. I kept the volume low on the computer in the small dressing area next to our bedroom. I had seen *Titanic* when it first came out in 1997, but hadn't seen it since and had no recollection of the song. Even after hearing it through a few times, it didn't ring a bell.

"My Heart Will Go On" is a pretty song, sweetly flowing, moderately catchy. Not my kind of music, but it clearly struck a chord with lots of people…the video has 92 million views on YouTube!

"Honey, is that Celine Dion?"

"Yes. Sorry for the noise."

"Why?"

"Why what?"

"Why are you listening to Celine Dion at eleven o'clock?"

"I've got to whistle for some Chinese bigwig tomorrow morning, and apparently he's a fan of the theme song to *Titanic*."

"*Titanic?*"

"Yup. I'll explain tomorrow."

"Come to bed. Practice in the morning."

―――――――――

Dave Marchick is my boss, an intense, dogged leader with a knack for the unexpected and a dry, sassy wit.

To build bridges between Carlyle (our employer) and China, where we are major investors, several times Dave's team has hosted Chinese government and business leaders for several days of meetings with academics, Wall Street investors, and government officials. From morning until night it's go, go, go, so it's good to squeeze in some fun here and there. This trip, karaoke was the entertainment of choice. To me, karaoke is novelty, but in Asian cultures it is art.

The president of the Bank of China—the most senior banking official in a land of 1.3 billion people—was a Celine Dion fan. At times like this, I realize how American culture is so inextricably woven into the fabric of countries around the globe. I would have paid dearly to hear the president's rendition at the karaoke session, which was how Dave knew he liked the song.

Humans are complex. I'm fascinated by the nooks and crannies of people's personalities. I relish the opportunities to get a true glimpse of a person beyond what they are willing to reveal, or in the case of a public figure, what the media will portray. This was a perfect example. A Chinese banker who liked Celine Dion? Sounds bizarre, incongruous, and exotic. But was it, really? How about a financial PR guy who liked to whistle?

I've worked with enough senior government officials and billionaire bankers to know that for them, there's more to life than just power and money...at least for the ones I've gotten to know. I once asked an astronaut, who had just returned from space, what it was like being an astronaut. He said he pulled his pants on one leg at a time. In other words, he was just like everyone else…unique, each with our own quirks. He might have even liked Celine Dion—you just never know.

No alarm was needed the next morning. I awoke in a near panic. I don't have the best memory for people's names or dates, but there's a special place in my brain for tunes. I hoped that hearing Celine sing a few times before sleep would give me a head start by the time I woke up.

No luck there. I fired up the song on my iPad in the kitchen and started to cram. Over and over I watched, listened, and gently whistled along. Feeling fresh and newly determined, the song started to gel in my brain.

Day two of the Carlyle investor conference was calling. In my car at 6:45 in the morning, at the Ritz Carlton in downtown DC by 7:20, on the long staircase to the lower level ballrooms at 7:22, and in my seat at 7:27, in time for the kick-off panel of well-known political reporters and former White House insiders. With the 2012 presidential election fourteen months away and the Republicans struggling to find a nominee to challenge President Obama, the audience was keenly interested in what the pundits had to say.

However entertaining and informative it was, I was growing anxious. It's one thing to whistle notes; it's another to make music…really know it, own it, shape it, and enjoy the delivery. I pretty much knew the notes at this point, but I wasn't ready to make music.

The panel ended at 8:30 in the morning. Hundreds of people got up to caffeinate, eat, network, and check e-mails in the adjacent foyer. I speedily retired to a phone booth outside the restrooms in the rear hallway. This was about as close as I'd ever come to feeling like Superman. I parked in there and prayed that my iPad would be able to receive the signal from YouTube and that I could rehearse without attracting attention. Anyone peeking through the clear glass window of the phone booth would have seen a forty-eight year-old man in suit and bowtie huddled over the gauzy image of Celine Dion singing of love as images of icebergs, terrified passengers, and gushing water wafted by, all the while whistling along. Who invited this guy to the Carlyle investor conference? Though I was surrounded by 800 people possessing or managing trillions of dollars, desperate times called for desperate measures.

Normally, I love to rehearse. It's peaceful and intense. It's wonderful alone time. It's where I stop reacting and start anticipating. It's transformative, where growth and progress are palpable. It's where I confront my musical weaknesses and figure out how to overcome them or create work-arounds. Take Hummel's Trumpet Concerto, for example. There's a section that I cannot duplicate (trumpets can do some things that lips can't), so when I perform it, I do some jazz improvisation instead. Purists might grimace at such a change, but whistling a trumpet concerto is so unorthodox to begin with that ninety-nine percent fidelity to the notes is enough.

Usually, I have weeks or even months to prepare for gigs and competitions. Now I had a final forty-five minutes to get my act together, to go from ignorance to bliss. At this point, I was focused on truncating the song from four minutes to under two while retaining the main themes.

Anyone who's ever sung along with their favorite song on the radio knows what it's like to sing a cappella. Take away the music or the words, and the crutch is gone, usually with messy results. Though I was now able to whistle the main theme and the refrain in sync with Celine, and had done so a few dozen times combined over the previous twelve hours, there would be no back-up music or accompaniment when it was time to serenade the president of the Bank of China. Since this was one of his favorite songs, he'd know right away if I missed any notes.

For the remaining fifteen minutes of my phone booth rehearsal, I focused on solo renditions. This is the challenging part of rehearsing, going from notes to music, that point at which the emphasis on each note diminishes and the phrase dominates, just as words meld into sentences and sentences into paragraphs.

In my view, whether you're a musician or public speaker (and I know plenty of both), it's all about what point you're trying to make. A proper musical performance takes the audience on a journey, telling stories along the way. I also like to tell stories in words, which has helped my musical storytelling and entertaining ability. My story here was one of love, how it transcends time and space. That's a heavy lift.

With five minutes left, it clicked. I had shortened and arranged the sections into a tight package that flowed well, and I could do it a cappella. I was ready, but that didn't mean I wasn't nervous.

I'm often asked if I get nervous before performing. "Of course," I always retort. It's good to be a little nervous before subjecting an audience to your singing, speechifying, or ukulele playing. Simply put, nerves are a sign of respect for the audience, and help to ensure you'll be well-prepared.

Too much nervousness, meanwhile, is toxic. It's like a wet blanket over an audio speaker, taking a dynamic sound and muffling it. Like a horse that senses the experience level of riders, audiences know when performers are at ease, in command, and enjoying themselves.

My senior year in college, I went to a piano recital. A graduate musical student was performing Schumann's *Fantasy in C*, a complex piece I knew well. She started confidently, asserting herself with clear understanding of the notes and music. But something happened during a tricky section. Her shoulders stiffened, and her hands struggled to find the path. The mood turned—lots of wrong notes. The joy was gone. She limped along to the end. I felt her pain.

For me, preparation is the key to managing nerves. The better prepared I am, the better I perform and the more fun I have, and presumably, the happier the audience is. In this case, I wished I'd had a little more time to prepare, but I was feeling good and ready to go.

In the cab ride over to the U.S. Chamber of Commerce, where the delegation was meeting, I did a little half-whistle half-hum of the tune. It was quite a turn-around from how I'd felt that morning.

It was a mild, sunny day. The Chamber, as it's known to Washington insiders, is at the corner of 16ᵗʰ and H Street, NW, across from La-fayette Park and a stone's throw from the White House (not that toss-ing stones in that direction is advisable). It's always special to see the White House, so stately and grand, regardless of who occupies it. As I exited the cab, I gazed at the White House for a moment, my confi-dence rising with the recollection of my command performance for the president in 2001; hoping to channel the intensity and excitement of that moment, I went into this other presidential gig.

Ushered by a Chamber staffer into an august, high-ceilinged room, I took a seat along the periphery as a U.S. senator spoke to the forty or so government officials and senior executives of Chinese state-owned entities about the importance of working constructively with China, including encouraging cross-border investing.

The session ended. Executives stretched and refilled their small breakfast plates with fruit and scrambled eggs and topped off their tea and coffee cups before taking their seats again around the long conference table.

Once settled, Dave got the attention of the group, asking the pres-ident to come to our side of the conference table. I stood and took a deep breath. The ship was ready to sail; hopefully with a better out-come than the Titanic.

Through interpreters, Dave explained who I was and what was about to happen. The delay in Dave's English words reaching the president's ears in Chinese was funny.

"Mr. President, this is Chris Ullman. He runs communications at Carlyle, but he is also a four-time world whistling champion."

While Dave was speaking, the president's face was flat and unre-active. When the interpreter got to "whistling" the president's eyes widened and he smiled at me. This was a good sign.

Dave continued, "Chris has whistled in the White House, with sym-phony orchestras, at Carlyle events, and today he is going to whistle the theme song to *Titanic*."

Again, the same reserved expression until the word *Titanic,* in Chinese, reached his ears. You'd have thought he had won the Powerball lottery. Until that moment, I suspect a wave of cognitive dissonance had swept over his brain: *Hhhmmm…U.S. senator just spoke…ornate room in prestigious organization's headquarters…host is expert on finance and investing…his employer is one of the world's largest and most prominent asset managers…new person with glasses and bow tie works with host…is going to whistle for me…at me?*

Breathe in, lick lips, pucker up, blow gently. No turning back to port now.

When I whistle songs with words, I typically run through the words in my head to help with phrasing. In this case, the words had not joined the notes in my brain, so that crutch was unavailable, but my mind's eye did recall the iconic image of Kate Winslet and Leonardo DiCaprio on the bow of the Titanic soon before disaster struck. Not sure what good that recollection did for my rendition, but a few seconds into it, I hadn't crashed into any metaphorical icebergs.

Then I heard it—a tune coming from somewhere other than my lips. *My imagination? Some weird brain spasm caused by having listened to Celine crooning several dozen times in the past twelve hours?*

No. It was the president himself humming along with me—gently, sweetly, note for note, in sync.

As if the duet (my first with a Chinese banker) wasn't enough to make this already unusual situation that much stranger, when I opened my eyes (closed eyes are a bad habit I'm working on), I could hardly believe what I saw.

He was in a state of tranquility, eyes closed, his right arm raised, hand gently swaying, fingers slightly curled, humming joyfully.

That was it. Now I'd seen it all. The president of the Bank of China, a complete stranger, standing only a few feet away, was conducting as I serenaded him.

Don't screw up, I thought. *You'll ruin this man's life!*

But the song wasn't over yet. When performing, you always have to presume that someone knows the music as well as you do. So, as the notes left my lips and I heard his humming, I knew that there was no room for error. It was actually a little freaky—not just the humming, but the whole experience. Which is saying something, considering how many weird whistling experiences I've had.

As I finished, the last notes echoed off the high ceilings. The president and I both had smiles on our faces. Mine reflected relief, and his reflected joy. The delegation clapped as the president warmly shook my hand and thanked me in English. I returned the appreciation and stepped back, as my part of the program was over.

Turning away from the president, my eyes swept the room. Face after face was smiling. How many business meetings end with nearly everyone happy? It's perhaps the best part of performing for people. Whether it's actual enjoyment of the tune, or fascination at the unusual nature of the instrument, it's a delight to help make that happen.

I began to leave, but was called back by the president. In a gracious gesture, he gave me a gift. When I got back to the office, I was eager to see what treat awaited me. Inside the eighteen-inch long, ornate box was a lovely woven tapestry depicting a lake surrounded by mountains. A Chinese colleague said it was a famous lake in China that conferred good luck and a happy life to those who visited it. Based on his happy heart and warm demeanor, I suspected my new banker friend was well familiar with it.

Some say love is the universal language; I think it's music. If I had run into the president of the Bank of China outside his office on Madison Avenue in Manhattan or on Jianshe Road in Shenzhen, China, we would have been unable to communicate and likely continued on our journeys posthaste. Music, like no other language, bridges the gap between strangers. In the case of myself and the top banker from China, it was whistling and a love song by Celine Dion that bridged our language deficit and briefly tangled our hearts in the sweetest of ways.

A Whistle That Touches My Heart

Name: Tony Warnock
Home: Sedalia, CO
Job: Cowboy, CEO of Lost Valley Ranch
Tony's *Whistle*: Hiring philosophy
How I Know Tony: Beginning in 2012, my wife, children, and I have vacationed annually at Lost Valley Ranch, which is nestled in Colorado's Pike National Forest.

***Whistle* in Action:** Tony is a real live cowboy, and he's good at it. He rides horses with skill and grace, hunts deer and elk for food, knows the rhythms of the flora and fauna of his mountainous home, and, yes, has a collection of awesome hats, boots, and belt buckles. But Tony's *whistle* that has touched my life the most is his hiring philosophy. Employees at Lost Valley are hired based on character, and then trained to do specific jobs. It's a deceptively simple approach that has yielded tremendous results. In the five years we've gone to Lost Valley, all the staff we have encountered (hundreds over the years) have been engaging, polite, warm, professional, and great at their jobs. Emphasizing character over skill yields staff who go above and beyond, who do the right thing, and who are tough, creative, and industrious. Tony and his team can teach people to cook, clean, fix, maintain, and wrangle, but they can't teach them honor and integrity, or why hard work, excellence, and service matter. It was the mountains and horses that first attracted us to Lost Valley, but it's the remarkable staff that brings us back every year. For that, we have Tony Warnock to thank.

CHAPTER 13
Happy Birthday, Ted

"DAD, IT'S NANCY. Can you hear me okay?"

"Oh, hi dear."

"Dad, I'm here with my friend Chris. And Mary, Mike, and James are on too."

"That's nice."

"Chris is going to whistle for your birthday."

"He's going to what?"

"Chris is a champion whistler. He's going to whistle for you."

"Oh, okay."

It was Ted's 100th birthday, and his daughter Nancy wanted to mark the day in a special way. I was honored to be part of the celebration.

My heart has a special place for seniors. They have this amalgam of wisdom and peace, nestled in the shadow of diminished relevance and failing health. Like gravity, life takes its toll.

Over the years, I've serenaded the parents of many work colleagues. Two stand out in my mind. Carlyle co-founder Bill Conway and Vice Chairman Dan Akerson had me whistle for their moms in their final years of life. It touched my heart to see these immensely successful businessmen look for a way to honor their moms with a simple gift that says "I love you" more than any fancy gift ever could.

In the years since, Bill and Dan have both mentioned how much these serenades meant to them. As my parents age (both are in their eighties), I better appreciate that time is fleeting and we need to honor and appreciate the special people in our lives while we can.

Over the years, I've whistled for seventy-five, eighty, and ninety year-olds, but then there was Ted. I had never whistled for a 100 year-old. Heck, I had never even spoken to a fellow human who was 100 years old. When Nancy asked me if I'd whistle for her centenarian father, I was so excited. We planned it months in advance.

On the special day, Nancy gathered her siblings from around the country on a conference call. One sibling was with Ted at his home in Arizona, while Nancy and I were in my office at Carlyle, hovering above a speakerphone.

I whistled my standard version, kicking it off with a fun little trumpet voluntary and ending with "and many more." Everyone cheered and clapped. Ted was touched by the call.

In the scheme of things, it was rather simple. On the other hand, it was simply magical.

It kind of reminded me of why I so enjoyed the twenty-five Grateful Dead concerts I went to in the '80s and '90s. The Dead were all about the music—no fancy stages, no costume changes, no fireworks or over-the-top lighting. The music stood on its own, needing no support from superficial things.

It was Ted's 100th birthday, a feat accomplished by few. With the whistle serving as catalyst, children scattered to the winds came together to honor their dear father. It wasn't elegant or lengthy, but it was delightful and heartfelt. When you're 100, I suspect that's just what the doctor ordered.

CHAPTER 14
Whistle While I Work

"When hearts are high the time will fly so whistle while you work."

"Whistle While You Work"

-Snow White and the Seven Dwarfs

SINCE 1992, I've worn bowties at work (tied myself, of course). I'm also partial to funky socks and pink shirts. So whistling at work is par for the course for someone who already pushes the limits in an executive suite that prizes uniform uniformity, literally and figuratively (think dark suits, white shirts, and Hermes ties, for the men at least).

I can't imagine what work would be like if I parked my whistle at home and studiously segregated the two. That said, I don't roam the halls mindlessly whistling a happy tune. That would drive my colleagues nuts. But my whistling is as much a part of me as my kinky hair and poor eyesight, so I whistle in the parking garage and stairwells, perform "Happy Birthday" in conference rooms, serenade my co-workers on their birthdays, deliver command performances at board meetings and company conferences, and always close my office door before delivering "Happy Birthdays" by phone to friends and family.

Today (the day I'm writing this chapter) is Carlyle Co-CEO Bill Conway's birthday. At some point today, I will either record a serenade for him or call his mobile and whistle. I like knowing when his birthday is, as well as his two fellow co-founders. It helps me relate to them better. It's a reminder that they are human and real and have feelings like all of us, despite their vaunted status as billionaires and global business leaders.

I think to a great extent, this is all about authenticity. How much of ourselves are we able and willing to bring to work? A lot depends on the culture of one's organization, but I think it's also about judiciously pushing boundaries. No one ever told me to whistle "Happy Birthday" for colleagues. It grew organically over time. The more I did it, the more I did it.

If I wasn't able to share my whistle with people, I'd feel like a fraud, especially in the workplace. That said, my title is Director of Global Communications, not bard or court musician. It's like anything in life: the key is to strike a balance between propriety and authenticity. I suspect this is the challenge that people in the LGBT community face, especially in a more staid corporate environment: How to be *you* without it getting in the way of the *job*.

The more people can bring their true selves to work, the more productive and happy they will be. That's especially true for me, because it's hard to be sad when whistling a happy tune. Happy employees equal greater productivity and, hopefully, increased profitability.

Whistling has always lifted my heart, whether I was walking down the street, delivering newspapers, building something in my workshop, or serenading a colleague at work. Music is like a drug for me, and whistling is an effective delivery device.

Thankfully, throughout my career, I've worked at places that welcome my whistling, so I could always be the real me. Nonetheless, to quote the Grateful Dead, "What a long strange trip it's been." In all my years of merging my day job with my whistle, none was as bizarre as when I interviewed for a job at a federal agency.

I was ushered into the spacious corner office of Arthur Levitt, chairman of the U.S. Securities and Exchange Commission, for my make-or-break job interview. At stake was whether I would become the top spokesman for the government body that oversees the stock markets and protects investors.

The chairman walked behind his large desk, littered with piles of paper. I stood on the opposite side, beside a chair. A moment before I was about to lower myself into the chair, Arthur told me I was one of two finalists…"So, please…whistle."

In the three seconds between hearing this crazy demand (coyly couched as a request), and delivering as ordered, an avalanche of thoughts crashed through my brain.

In retrospect, it reminded me of a dreamy scene in the Broadway play *Hamilton*. For ninety seconds, time stands still between the moment Aaron Burr fires his gun and when the bullet hits Hamilton in the most famous duel in American history. In that time, as Hamilton realizes he's about to die, he has flashbacks and flash-aheads, examining his life and even looking forward to seeing cherished souls (his mother, son, George Washington, and John Laurens) who preceded him to the grave.

While my time-standing-still moment involved a far cheerier subject, it was still cognitive dissonance defined. *How could this be happening? Surely it isn't possible that I was just told to whistle in a job interview, and not for just any PR job, but to be spokesman for a federal agency. What, no foreplay…just launch into a performance with no warm-up or discussion? Is this a test? Should I tell him "no" and show my good judgment, or just belt out a tune and show my flexibility and courage? What tune can possibly capture the audacity of the moment? And what if I screw up? Why is he staring at me with those piercing blue eyes? What's up with that wry smile? How does he even know I whistle? Do I look like a deer in the headlights right now? This is crazy. Is it over yet?*

Thankfully, brains are spectacularly fast multi-processors, because in those three seconds, a solution emerged that saved the day. *Arthur likes opera!* (During the interview process, someone had randomly mentioned that Arthur was an opera fan.) *I know some opera!* (There's some opera on the *120 Music Masterpieces* albums I listened to all the time as a kid.) *How's that tune go?* (Silently sing the words and the tune will come.)

Trying to suppress surprise, and not having time to get even more nervous (this was a job interview, after all), I did as ordered and began to whistle the aria "Vesti la giubba" from the opera *Pagliacci* by Ruggero Leoncavallo. Though this piece hadn't passed through my lips in several years, the tune was etched into my brain from years of whistling it as a kid. In this clutch moment, I somehow dusted off the cobwebs, determined where to start, and let the notes flow. I even had some fun with it. Arthur wanted a performance, and I gave him one, replete with swaying body and hand gestures.

I can't remember a word of our ensuing conversation—all I know is that I got the job. He provoked, and I delivered.

Presumably, Arthur had already concluded I could do the job; the real question was how I'd perform under pressure. That's usually a tough one to judge in a job interview, but, as I would soon learn as his spokesman, Arthur was anything but typical.

During the four years I worked for Arthur, I learned many important lessons about work and life. One was that people aren't commodities. As a student of human nature, Arthur is very good at pinpointing a person's special abilities and traits. That's why, I believe, he had me whistle. He had actually read to the end of my resume, where in the "Interests" section, I listed competitive whistling. That must have piqued his interest. So, Arthur, being Arthur, put me to the test. It was probably my first introduction to the concept of finding one's *whistle*. Arthur helped me identify my *whistle*, in the most unorthodox of ways.

That I whistled on my job interview got around pretty quickly; even if I had wanted to downplay my puckered pursuits, I was doomed from day one. In my four years at the SEC, I effectively became a minstrel, whistling at many-a-birthday party. I established a nice rhythm; my hobby and my day job were seamlessly merged. People respected me for my PR counsel *and* they enjoyed the whistling. Much had to do with the good-spirited people I worked with, and it helped that I always remembered that I was working in a highly professional regulatory and enforcement agency known for being a serious place.

After winning the grand championship in 1999, I asked Arthur if he was okay with me giving a concert for the SEC staff. True to form, he thought it was a great idea and gave his imprimatur. I had no idea how many people would show up for a free lunch-time whistling concert, a Commission first. To my utter shock and delight, there was standing room only in the Commission's formal main meeting room.

A nice buzz filled the room, unlike the more serious whispers that preceded a typical meeting in this space. Some attendees knew what they were in for, though I wondered how many had just seen the concert posters around the Commission and thought it would be fun to see the freaky carnival sideshow.

My pianist and I perched in front of the dais that the commissioners presided from when enforcing and regulating. A senior colleague introduced us, and then we launched into an upbeat "Take the 'A' Train," which got the crowd fired up. I talked a little, but mostly whistled. The highlight of the performance was a medley of improvised blues tunes named after SEC regulations. It doesn't get any geekier than that. The lawyers and accountants ate it up.

I learned an incredible lesson that day: the power of truly embracing one's role. As a non-actor, this was new to me. Sure, over the course of my day job and whistling careers I had done lots of public speaking and performing. In those situations, though, I was either PR guy talking about PR, or the whistler whistling. This, however, was the PR guy whistling a full concert in front of colleagues, who were also my clients. Straddling these two worlds has often been a challenge, like when I whistle "Happy Birthday" to officemates. Yes, I'm the PR guy whistling at work, but under those circumstances, I feel like I'm just whistling and not performing. There's a big difference.

Performing is all about engagement with the audience, being in the moment, body motions, and eye contact. When I whistle at work, I have little to none of that stuff. I let the whistle honor the birthday boy or girl, not me, and that works well. But that approach doesn't work in a fifty minute concert. It would be come across as stiff and awkward.

So, as I got up in front of lots of serious lawyer and accountant colleagues, I decided that I'd be *Chris the Whistler* and not *Chris the PR Guy Who Happens to Whistle*. It was liberating. Embracing my role helped me engage more deeply with the audience, looking right into people's eyes as I whistled, freely telling stories and having fun. It was more about me than I'm used to, but audiences expect that. They viewed me as a means of delight, and I viewed them as a group to be wooed. It was a perfect match.

The concert was a smashing success. The audience of several hundred reveled in this momentary respite from their serious day jobs, clapping and laughing. People talked about it for weeks. I had a great time, and it didn't hurt my career at the Commission. Eighteen years later, I still have warm feelings from that special day.

That lesson about the power of playing the role has had a big impact on my PR and whistling careers. It's enabled me to be more purposeful with each, especially when the two have intersected.

Speaking of intersections, I'm fascinated by the total unpredictability of lips and day jobs crashing together. In the fall of 2012, Dave Marchick and I had just finished a presentation to Carlyle's board of directors. Carlyle had become a public company a few months before, and this was my first meeting with the board. Pleased that our time with the directors had gone well, Dave and I gathered our stuff and prepared to leave the room, when out of the blue, Carlyle co-founder and Chairman Dan D'Aniello announced that in addition to being head of communications, "Chris has a special talent: he's a champion whistler."

I kept walking toward the door, hoping this declaration would not get traction, but Dan insisted on a demonstration. He asked me what song I would do. I hesitated a moment, trying to figure out an appropriate song for the audience and circumstances. As I pondered, Dan decided.

"How about 'Stars and Stripes Forever?'"

A big fan of John Phillip Sousa, the military march king, I felt good about that. With no time to warm up or practice the challenging piece, I mustered a passable performance to the delight of Dan and at least some of the board. One board member was so tickled by my patriotic injection into the otherwise appropriately staid meeting that we have become friends and I have added her to my birthday whistle list.

Another out-of-the-blue command office performance also led to a nice outcome. Beavering away in my office one day, the phone rang; it was David Rubenstein's assistant, summoning me to a conference room beside his office.

Upon arrival, David introduced me to his guest, Ted Leonsis, a businessman, entrepreneur, former executive at AOL, and owner of Washington's professional basketball and hockey teams, the Wizards, Mystics, and Capitals.

This turned out to be a dual function meeting: whistling first, business second. With an impish tone, David said that Ted was interested in my whistling. Within a few minutes of chatting, Ted said he'd be happy to have me perform the national anthem at one of his team's games. Just like that. I didn't even have to audition.

That was a first. From what little I knew about Ted, I was not surprised that he would think a whistled national anthem would be pretty cool. What I knew came from newspaper features over the years and an interview Ted did with David Rubenstein at the Economic Club of Washington, D.C. a few years before.

In that interview, Ted spoke about his new book, *The Business of Happiness*. He talked wistfully, even lovingly, about his 101-item bucket list, which was filled with disparate, seemingly out-of-character things, a sign of a curious mind. One by one, he was checking off items, from making a movie to writing a book to starting a business. I thought it would be fascinating to one day meet this man and learn more about his philosophy. Now, without fanfare, in David's conference room, I saw first-hand that zest for life and the twinkle in his eye that allows someone to be open to an oddity like whistling.

It was a brief, but inspiring, encounter, and it led to an awesome outcome, performing the national anthem to an unsuspecting but appreciative audience of 20,000 or so at the Verizon Center in downtown

DC. Never before was I so at peace and in command of my instrument while honoring our nation.

We did go on to talk about a business idea Ted had, which David charged me with exploring. It was fascinating, switching gears so quickly; meeting an iconic entrepreneur, getting a highly sought-after gig, and then discussing actual business.

Years before, I was with another curious mind who had a very different reaction. It was 1996, and it took place in an elevator on Capitol Hill.

My boss, House Budget Committee Chairman John Kasich, and I were coming back from a meeting on the Senate side of the Capitol when we crossed paths with Speaker of the House Newt Gingrich. The two of them started chatting about the latest budget negotiation with the White House. Along with the Speaker's omnipresent bodyguard, we got in an elevator. John said, "Newt, this is my press secretary, Chris Ullman. He's a world champion whistler."

Silence.

"He's been on *The Tonight Show*."

No reaction.

The elevators on Capitol Hill are rather small, so the awkwardness, for me at least, was palpable. I looked for sympathy in the eyes of the big guy with the gun (Newt's security detail), but he belied not a shred of acknowledgment. His job was to keep people's hands, and if need be, lips away from the Speaker. I clenched my jaw and stared at the floor, not wanting to antagonize the third-highest ranking person in the U.S. government. Undeterred by his volley not returned, John pivoted to the ongoing budget negotiations. Door opened. Breathing resumed.

Things may not have always worked out well with the politically powerful, but they went much better with the rich. In my fifteen years at Carlyle, I've performed several times at our annual investor conference in Washington, DC, a gathering of nearly 1,000 institutional investors and wealthy individuals.

The event is hosted at the National Building Museum, one of the grandest and most beautiful buildings in Washington. It regularly houses presidential inaugural galas, charitable fundraisers and corporate events. With a 100-foot ceiling supported by eight five-foot diameter columns, whether you're a guest or speaker, it's awe-inspiring grandeur.

The first time, in 2002, a year after I started working at Carlyle, David Rubenstein came up to me during the dinner and asked if I'd like to whistle. I was still getting to know David at that point, and was shocked that he'd take such a risk. Having your PR guy warm up for the headline performer (in this case, the famous Tony Bennett) in front of an audience of people who manage trillions of dollars, without giving the meeting planner or the whistler a heads up, seemed pretty radical. That entrepreneurial spirit is at the core of David's success.

I was stunned, humbled, and *petrified*. If you blow a performance, you embarrass yourself. It's a whole 'nother thing to embarrass your boss. Thankfully, I didn't have much time to get nervous. Within twenty minutes, David mounted the stage, hushed the crowd, welcomed them to the event, and presented his special treat for the evening—me.

I stood before the large audience, whistling Duke Ellington's "Take the 'A' Train." Since I was performing without accompaniment, I needed a song that was upbeat, fun, would work with an international audience, and provide some "wow" factor. "Take the 'A' Train" is one of those songs that everyone knows or everyone likes the first time they hear it. It always gets a good audience reaction.

Good song selection, solid performance, happy audience, happier boss, employment maintained. That must have emboldened David, because four other times over the years, he has had me serenade our investors at that big annual event at the same grand venue. The second to last time, in 2015, was the best and most memorable, and I learned a powerful lesson.

This time, ten minutes before the event started, David approached me and asked what I was going to whistle. Though I should have known better, I actually thought he was kidding. It had been several years since my last command performance, and I'd believed he had moved on from injecting my lips into the event.

Wrong.

"You didn't mention this before," I said, my concern obvious.

"Are you scared?"

I'm not a billionaire, but I'm competitive, so his challenge would be properly answered. "I'm not scared, I just like to be prepared."

"What's your hardest song?" he asked.

No time to waste, I stood up and we started walking quickly in the direction of the stage. I said, "Give me five minutes. I need to work something out with the band."

Thankfully, I had previously performed with the band leader, Glenn Pearson, a stunningly talented pianist, who was tickling the ivories with his ensemble when I arrived a few moments after David threw down the gauntlet. Glenn saved the day by suggesting a patriotic medley: "Yankee Doodle," and "You're a Grand Old Flag," with "The Battle Hymn of the Republic" as the finale. For thirty seconds we ran through tempos and key changes, and then it was pencils down.

David gaveled the dinner to order, introduced me, and off we patriotically went.

It was a true "in the moment" performance. I've never felt so alive as a performer. I wasn't constrained by what I had rehearsed, because I hadn't beaten any notes or riffs into my brain in advance. Instead, I whistled what I felt at the moment. Glenn, an attentive accompanist, was there with me note for note. The audience was enthralled, with applause and hoots coming throughout our three-minute jaunt…not something you'd expect from a group of serious businesspeople.

"Battle Hymn" sent the audience over the edge. We went slow gospel to upbeat jazzy, modulating through two higher keys as we neared the finale. With a high note dusted with a little vibrato, it was over. The audience of financial bigwigs erupted in applause. I smiled, relieved, and raised a hand in acknowledgement.

It was one of my favorite performances ever, and a smashing success, based on the feedback I got. Person after person, for several days, expressed how delightful, joyous, and unbounded it was.

That's the great lesson. In life, be prepared, but don't over-rehearse to the point of constriction. Audiences can tell the difference, feel the difference. It's the difference between good and great. It's why live performances can be so much fun, so satisfying, for artist and audience.

From that high, a chance meeting in the office brought me back down to earth. Beavering away one day, a familiar face walked passed my open office door. As if a doctor had struck my vocal chords with a hammer, I reflexively yelled his name.

"Tucker!"

One moment passed, then another. Somewhat sheepishly, a tall frame topped with a shaggy brown mane returned. "Yes?" His tentativeness demonstrated that he had no idea who I was.

I quickly stood up and moved around my desk toward him, extending my hand. "Tucker, I'm Chris Ullman, the whistler. I was on your show a couple of years ago."

The light of acknowledgement brightened his eyes.

"I have a bone to pick with you."

The light dimmed a bit as his eyes narrowed.

Tucker Carlson, conservative thinker, writer, and commentator, had a political talk-show on MSNBC for several years. As had happened to me many times over the years with this or that TV or cable show, I got a random call from his producer, asking if I'd like to be a guest on his show.

Always eager to share my whistle and show off a bit, I said sure, that would be great. In preparing for the interview, I learned that Tucker was a Grateful Dead fan. I offered to whistle a Dead tune, and the producer loved it. Rather than give Tucker a heads up, the producer suggested I just whistle the tune when asked to demonstrate my talent. The producer suggested "Bird Song," one of Tucker's favorites, which was fine with me.

At that time, Tucker's show aired quite late. My segment, which was live, was after eleven at night. The late hour notwithstanding, I kept my energy up and the interview went well...he loved my rendition of "Bird Song." It was a little awkward because we were in different studios; he was in New York, and I was in DC. That's why he hadn't recognized me when he walked past my door.

"Why, what did I do?" he asked as we stood there in my office.

Not too long after I was on his show, network brass moved his show from the late hour to prime time. His wit and intellect had led to strong ratings, which warranted a better time slot.

Good for him. Bad for me.

Soon after he went prime time, I started getting phone calls and e-mails from friends saying that they had seen me on Tucker's new show, this time in not such a flattering way. On one of his first shows, he did a segment on guests he'd had on his show when it aired late in the evening who would no longer be welcome now that he was prime time. Sure enough, there I was.

Standing a few feet apart in my office, mano-a-mano, I pointed out how he had dissed me once he went prime time. In the finest Washington spin-meister tradition (it takes one to know one), he did what any self-respecting politician would do; he blamed his producer!

I wasn't upset, I just wanted to yank his chain and make him squirm a bit, the way pundits make politicians squirm. The conversation quickly moved to why he was roaming the halls of Carlyle. He and a partner were looking to start a conservative news website, and were seeking ideas and advice from a colleague of mine. Soon after, Tucker launched *The Daily Caller*, and it's been prime time ever since.

Not resting on his laurels, David Rubenstein continued to encourage me to take my whistling to new heights, in this case quite literally. On a bright summer day, he suggested a performance that was unlike any other in my long whistling career.

"When you get to the top, you should whistle "Yankee Doodle." That's probably never happened before." David said, as we gazed up at the 555-foot tall Washington Monument, the centerpiece of the National Mall.

In high school, on a family trip to DC, I had taken the elevator to the top of the Washington Monument, but this imminent assault would be quite different. We were about to scale the *exterior* scaffolding enshrouding the monument, which had been damaged in a 2011 earthquake and kept shuddered since. David was funding half the $15 million repair costs, so the National Park Service offered to take him on a tour of the project. As his trusty PR guy, I got to tag along.

I walked up the 500 foot high staircase to the point where the pyramid of the obelisk began. The views were spectacular, breathtaking and knee-shaking. Familiar objects looked different, grander, from the new vantage point. Walking around the monument at the 500-foot level, my eyes took in the U.S. Capitol to the east, Reagan Airport in Virginia to the south, the stately World War II and Lincoln Memorials to the west, and the White House to the north.

A worker hooked a rope to my safety harness, and up the sixty foot ladder I climbed. Along the way, I passed one of four giant red lights, each more than a foot in diameter, which warn aircraft that a building (in this case a massive obelisk) is nearby. As a longtime Washington resident, I had seen these pulsating red lights countless times from a great distance at night. Now I was eye-to-eye with one of them, something I'd never envisioned happening. I reached out and touched the red glass. It felt intimate and adventurous, like I was poking a monster in the eye.

Ten feet later, I passed through a twenty-four inch square opening and emerged on the top of the world...the political one, at least. The platform at the top was no more than six feet wide. At 555 feet, the monument dwarfs everything around it. A plane landing at Reagan National flew by at the same level. Even though I'm usually unafraid of heights, this time my legs were wobbly.

Protruding from the plywood platform was the very top of the obelisk, the last three feet or so of the marble stone topped off with a foot-high mini-pyramid made of aluminum, a metal so difficult to fabricate, it was considered precious in the late nineteenth century.

I knelt down, and holding tight to the marble, kissed the aluminum and whistled "Yankee Doodle." It was a surreal experience, towering above my home of twenty-six years, in a place few humans have gone, serenading the spirit of our iconic hero president.

A Whistle That Touches My Heart

Name: Kelly Burkart
Home: Apple Valley, MN
Job: Web writer and consultant
Kelly's *Whistle*: Handmade Christmas cards
How I Know Kelly: In 1994, I worked for U.S. Representative Rod Grams (R-MN). Kelly was an intern in our Washington, DC office.

***Whistle* in Action**: Come into the Ullman kitchen in the month of December, and you'll see lots of Christmas and holiday cards attached to festive ribbons hanging in front of the windows overlooking our backyard. They are a reminder of the importance of the season and the love of family and friends. I appreciate them all, but amidst all the representations of the Madonna, snowflakes, baby Jesus, and freshly-scrubbed smiling kids, you'll find a card that particularly warms my heart. For as long as I can remember, Kelly Burkart has sent us a handmade Christmas card. It's the only one constructed piece-by-piece, using stamps, hand-cut paper, and glue-on embellishments. It's the card I most look forward to each year. Our mutual exchange of Christmas cards with enclosed holiday family letters has been our only means of communications for nearly twenty years, until I called her recently. It was nice to hear her sweet Minnesota lilt after all those years. She told me, "I've always loved crafts, and making cards has been a great hobby because there's a tangible result that makes other people happy." Every year she makes about 100 Christmas cards, and we are the happy beneficiaries of her handmade gift.

CHAPTER 15

Happy Birthday, Virginia

"HELLO?"

"Hi. Is this the birthday girl?"

Laughing, she says she can't believe I remembered.

"I was looking forward to this day," I said

"Do you know where I am?" she replied. Before I could even answer, she declared that she was in Tibet, at the foot of Mount Everest.

"They have cell coverage there?" I asked incredulously. It sounded like she was next door.

We chatted for a moment about her trip. She was touring the area, not preparing an assault on the 29,029 foot tall mountain. Not sure of what this was costing her, I asked if she was ready for a serenade.

There was a sweet eagerness in her voice that warmed my heart, knowing I was competing with monumental majesty and grandeur.

I did my best to deliver a celebration of life that matched the moment.

It was a fleeting encounter, but with lasting effects, on me at least. What a special joy to reach around the world and add to Virginia's special day, which was already about as special as you can get. Everest! Mount Everest. Wow!

Virginia and I ran into each other several months later, and she filled me in on her trip. The whistle, she said, was the icing on the cake to an amazing experience.

CHAPTER 16
So What Are the Notes?

"HOW WOULD YOU like to perform with the National Symphony Orchestra?"

Was I dreaming? Nope—but it was a dream come true.

Elizabeth Schulze, the associate director of the NSO, had actually just asked if I'd like to whistle with her orchestra. It's not like I badgered her into it; the idea was hers.

It was like getting the "fat" envelope, indicating acceptance to the university you had always dreamed of attending. I said yes before I even knew what she had in mind. Pesky details.

Elise Neal, a friend and fellow fan of the NSO, had invited me to see the orchestra perform at Wolf Trap, the only national park dedicated to the performing arts, located in Vienna, Virginia.

Vivacious and quite a talker, Elise was also volunteer president of the young adult support group FANS—Friends Assisting the National Symphony. Our encounter with the conductor was at a post-concert reception that FANS members were invited to. Also an energetic marketer, Elise practically dragged me over to meet Elizabeth and immediately launched into a pitch on my unusual talent. Elise definitely "got it" when it came to the whistling. She thought it was quirky, fun, and worthy.

Director Schulze, pumped from her performance only minutes

earlier, seemed game. She was pleasant and welcoming, and within minutes, broached the subject of me whistling for her. She was a bit sheepish, probably torn between respect and curiosity. If I were an opera singer, there's no way she would have asked me to belt out a few notes. But I wasn't an opera singer; I was a whistler. Thankfully, I was used to doing command performances, though at times I've felt like a trained monkey, asking "How high?" when people said "Jump." Worse things in life have happened.

"I feel bad putting you on the spot, but could you whistle a little?"

Hmmm, let me check my schedule. "Sure, I'd be happy to."

I cranked out a little "In the Mood" by Glenn Miller, at the time a favorite of mine that shows how versatile whistling can be.

Her face alive, Elizabeth immediately looked at the person next to her—the executive director of the symphony—then turned back to me, saying they needed to talk in private for a moment. She and the director stepped several feet away.

Elise and I looked at each other, wondering what this meant. It certainly wasn't bad, but neither of us could have predicted what happened next.

Returning a few moments later, a Cheshire grin barely contained, Elizabeth got right to the point: would I like to perform with the NSO?

O.M.G!!

At the upcoming Labor Day concert at the U.S. Capitol, she said, the NSO was going to perform a song written for a whistler, but had planned on having members of the orchestra whistle it—that is, anyone whose mouth wasn't already busy blowing into some instrument. It being a reception and her being the star, time was short, so we exchanged contact info and my first big-time orchestra debut was on the calendar.

Elise and I looked at each other and hugged. I thanked her profusely for making the introduction. What a testament to being in the right place at the right time, and the power of making life happen, rather than waiting around hoping. For Elise, this was par for the course. That's what people like her do.

Three years before, I had set a goal of performing with symphony orchestras in general, and the NSO in particular.

In college, I started listening to Mozart's Oboe Concerto, a delightful piece filled with rollercoaster runs and catchy tunes. (A concerto is a solo instrument plus orchestra.) At around twenty-two minutes long, it was a marathon of notes. Almost by osmosis, though, I learned to whistle it. Over and over, I worked on the complex sections, and eventually could whistle the whole piece note for note.

One day, it popped in my head: *wouldn't it be amazing to perform this piece with a symphony orchestra?* A duel in my mind began.

Of course it would be cool.

Whistling is frivolous, while symphonies are serious.

Nothing ventured, nothing gained.

Spend your time and money on something achievable.

But this would be totally cool!

What right-minded conductor would feature a whistler with his or her orchestra, especially performing Mozart?

Well, I was about to find out. With the help of Bob Devaney, a DJ at WETA, the classical public radio station in Washington, DC, I made a demo tape. I then found and purchased a directory of all the orchestras in the U.S., selected fifty in the DC metropolitan area, large and small, wrote a pitch letter, and off went the packages.

In the letter, I acknowledged the artistic and financial risks of performing with a whistler, offsetting it with the seriousness of my approach plus the need for orchestras to try new things in order to expand their audience base.

Most ignored me. A few said thanks, but no thanks. To my utter shock and delight, two said yes. One was the McLean Symphony Orchestra, located in nearby McLean, VA, and the other was the Mary Washington College Symphony Orchestra in Fredericksburg, VA.

I had sent a package to the National Symphony Orchestra and followed up with phone calls, but couldn't get any traction. Hence, my deep satisfaction and amazement when Elizabeth asked me to perform with the NSO.

The real take-away is that life is not linear. It's quite crooked, filled with peaks and valleys. Obstacles abound. Rarely do life's greatest and most exciting journeys subscribe to the geometric rule that the shortest distance between two points is a straight line.

There's an expression at Carlyle, "hanging around the hoop." It simply means that you never write off an opportunity after having been rebuffed. Sometimes the ball bounces in your direction when you least expect it, which means you should always prepare for, and even seek, the unexpected. Put yourself in the right position, and good things will happen, eventually. My performances with those two other orchestras went well. I learned a lot, which helped prepare me for my big NSO gig.

A few days after I was awarded the gig of a lifetime, I was at work on Capitol Hill and on the phone with Director Schulze. She had faxed me the sheet music and was humming me through it, with me humming it back to make sure we were in sync. Upon hanging up, my colleague Roger Mahan, seated a few feet away, blurted out, "1976 Republican nominating convention, as Ronald Reagan was approaching the stage to introduce Gerald Ford."

"Huh?"

"That's the music that was playing as Reagan was coming on stage."

"What stage? How did you know that?"

"C-SPAN has been replaying political conventions, and I've recorded them. The other day I was watching the 1976 convention, and I remember the tune."

Ya gotta love it, watching old political conventions for fun. What would the geeks of Washington do without C-SPAN? Well, imagine what sports nuts would do without ESPN and you get the idea. It wouldn't be pretty.

The song Roger remembered so well was composed in 1923 by Edwin Franko Goldman. "On the Mall" is a delightful march that would have made Sousa jealous. Though it was being performed on the National Mall in Washington, it was written in dedication of the Elkan Naumburg Bandshell in New York City's Central Park.

Over the next three weeks, I rehearsed one to two hours a day. Roger lent me the videotape of the Republican nominating convention as a whistle-along rehearsal tool. "On the Mall" is a wonderfully catchy tune, which made rehearsing fun. It started with a brief orchestra-only introduction, then I whistled four variations on the main theme, known as the trio section, as the orchestra receded in the background. We repeated the trio section, again with quiet orchestra. The finale was the trio section a third time, with the orchestra at full-fledged forte... delightfully loud! All-in, the song was just over three minutes.

I've long thought the song has the potential to be the next "Don't Worry, Be Happy," the one-hit wonder by Bobby McFerrin, which took the world by storm in 1988. All it needs is a delightful arrangement and brilliant marketing, plus a full moon and a miracle!

It could be the song that brings whistling back to the public consciousness and lips, where it hasn't been probably since the start of the Cold War. Whistlers are stuck between this idealized version of the past and a bleak assessment of the future. One more project to add to my list.

The morning of the concert, I walked from my home on Capitol Hill to the foot of the U.S. Capitol to rehearse with the orchestra. It was a beautiful late summer day, nothing like the swampy heat of July and August that Washington is infamous for.

I had seen the NSO perform many times at its home at the John F. Kennedy Center for the Performing Arts as well as at the U.S. Capitol, so standing *with* the musicians as a fellow performer made me giddy. At the same time, I had a mild case of Imposter Syndrome, wondering if I even belonged up there with them.

Too late for that, I concluded, *the show must go on.*

Watching the orchestra rehearse reminded me of the line from Clement Clarke Moore's "A Visit from St. Nicholas" about St. Nick: "He spoke not a word, but went straight to his work."

Piece after piece, the orchestra followed the steady baton of Director Schulze, no theatrics or fuss. A few times she stopped them mid-section to make an adjustment, but otherwise they went straight to their work. That's the beauty of a classical music concert. It doesn't need fancy lighting or costumes. It's all about being great conveyors, playing notes and channeling the mood and vision of the composer while enjoying a touch of artistic license.

Well, for them to go straight to their work made perfect sense, as that's what they did day in and day out. For me, on the other hand, literally standing in the midst of a cranked up seventy-piece symphony orchestra was simply amazing, otherworldly, overwhelming. The sound was enveloping and permeating. It was all around me and in me and wonderfully loud. I heard the orchestra as never before. It was like adding quality speakers to a stereo after years of the crappy built-in ones. Finally, I could associate each instrument with its unique sound: the silky smooth violins, the breathy clarinets, the nasally oboes, and the thunderous timpani.

My dream to perform with the NSO was happening, and it was more joyous than I had exuberantly imagined. I tried to contain my delight and nonchalantly take my place on the rehearsal conveyor belt. Soon, my turn came. I walked on stage, the conductor introduced me, I greeted the concertmaster, she raised her baton, the orchestra played, I whistled the right notes at the right time, and then we were finished. One and done, the rehearsal was over before I knew it. All appeared to go well, or so the absence of snickering from the wind section would seem to indicate. With that hurdle cleared, my confidence was rising. All was good.

A few days before the rehearsal, Director Schulze asked me what I thought of teaching the audience how to whistle the song. I'd whistle it alone with the orchestra at the beginning of the concert, and then come back near the end, teach the assembled masses the song, and then conduct them through it with the orchestra. I was in.

At the rehearsal, the concertmaster, William Steck, and I came up with a plan. I'd tell the audience what we were going to do, William and I would demonstrate each part of the trio section, me on lip, him on violin, and then we'd practice each part with the audience. It seemed like a good plan, but I wondered if we could pull it off. Getting 60,000 people to do anything in unison is challenging, let alone asking them to whistle a song they learned minutes before. This was going to be awesome.

I returned to the Capitol at six that evening. As a long-term Washington, DC resident, I have stood before the magnificent white dome countless times, but this time was different. Between the stunningly illuminated building and me was a sea of humanity, gathered for the annual Labor Day concert. Colorful blankets sat upon by casually dressed residents and tourists littered the west lawn. A few Frisbees streaked back and forth. In previous years, that was me playing Frisbee with friends before enjoying a picnic and music. Seeing so many people made me question the viability of this audience participation idea. Director Schulze didn't seem phased.

While worrying about the end, a near-disaster occurred at the beginning of my performance. The sun hung low in the sky, and the west facing front of the Capitol was buttery yellow in the warm light. The stage manager cued me as the audience applause wound down from the preceding piece. There was no written program, so who knew how many people heard the announcer say that the accompanist on the next piece was a whistler?

This is it, I thought. The die was cast. All the rehearsing and pondering and praying had come down to this. I was nervous. I was ready. I was about to get what I had long sought: a gig with a major symphony orchestra. Be careful what you wish for.

Lord, please bless me, I pleaded.

I walked on stage and sat on a chair a few feet from the conductor. Elizabeth raised her baton, and the first notes of "On the Mall" marched across the huge audience.

"On the Mall" is the kind of song you can't help but like the first time you hear it. That's the beauty of a march; you just want to get up and go.

Twenty seconds into the orchestral introduction, I stood and approached the microphone, surveying the audience. Then I looked up at the Capitol dome; its stark brightness contrasted brilliantly against the darkening sky. I was in awe. I was overwhelmed. I was being consumed by the pressure of the moment.

With seconds left before my entrance, I realized my mind was blank. The notes were gone.

How could this happen after so much rehearsal? I thought, as an infusion of some chemical jabbed my stomach.

The conductor looked directly into my eyes, raised her baton, and gave the cue.

Notes come out. They sounded familiar. I was on autopilot, not a good place for a performer to be. The crowd, Capitol, and orchestra conspired to overwhelm my senses and stir stage-fright angst that resided beneath the surface. Since I was a little kid, I've struggled against choking at the big moment. The only antidote is relentless preparation.

I had rehearsed, though. Maybe this experience was just too much.

Then, without warning, the autopilot was flipped off just as unexpectedly as it had arrived. Maybe it was five seconds, but it seemed like an eternity.

The same thing happened my first time skydiving. Despite hours of training on the ground, at the appointed moment, I forgot to pull the rip-chord. Thankfully, the nearby instructor remembered.

Once engaged, I had the time of my life. The next three minutes came and went too fast. From a performance perspective, I had hit the trifecta: a fun song in front of a massive crowd in an august setting. In my case, it was the first such triple-play, and could easily be the last, so I tried to enjoy every moment.

Several times Elizabeth and I locked eyes, especially during the quiet trio section, which better enabled the audience to hear the whistle. We were in sync. I wonder if she felt relief, knowing that I was a relatively unproven performer. She seemed to be enjoying herself too. Her smile gave me confidence. Her baton helped me deliver a crisp performance.

Five years later, I would have a near identical feeling while whistling for the president in the Oval Office, a palpable understanding that this was not normal and would likely never happen again. I was not Mick Jagger, who's made a career of crooning the night away in stadiums full of adoring fans. I was Chris, the public relations guy who occasionally whistles in unusual settings: the U.S. Capitol, the Oval Office, the top of the Washington Monument.

With a warbling flourish, it was over. In retrospect, I'm surprised I didn't collapse on the spot. Talk about tragedy narrowly averted.

The audience erupted in applause and hoots and whistles. They seemed to realize this was not the usual NSO performance. However unusual it was to have a whistler with their beloved orchestra, it worked, and it was fun.

Exiting the stage, I was a jumble of emotions—ecstasy at having nailed it, dread at having nearly blown it. I wondered whether putting myself in these stressful situations was worth it. *What if I had puckered up and the wrong notes came out?* I banished the thought; it was time to bask a bit. People were shaking my hand and offering high fives. It was a hit. I smiled and said thanks…no time for doubt or navel gazing. I needed to stay focused, as the gig was only half over, and the harder part was still to come.

A little more than an hour later, it was time for the mass teach-in and whistle. I walked back on stage and said, "The whistler speaks." I explained that I would teach them the four parts of the song with help from the concertmaster. William and I demonstrated each part. The audience quickly picked up the tune—but would they be able to piece the four parts together?

Again, the conductor gave the cue and the orchestra was marching along. At the right moment, with the right notes, I cued the audience, and one of the largest whistle-ins in history began—a remarkable 60,000 people all puckering and blowing along with one of the great symphonies in America.

The melodies, bouncing off the stone and iron of the Capitol walls and dome, swept across the broad lawn and filled my head and heart. With each verse, the collective confidence grew. We were making music. This was not your usual concert, where the audience is passive, clapping occasionally. They were listening and engaged, the only way possible to hear a song and re-create it on the spot.

The finale was amazing—orchestra at forte, audience in the groove, my amplified whistle intermingling with it all. *Could this feeling be bottled?*

I glanced down at some friends who were in the front row. They were standing, waving little signs that said: "I'm a Chris Ullman fan." That made my mind smile, as my lips were still busy whistling.

Then it was over.

With a bow and a wave, I was off the stage, and the most remarkable experience of my thirty-three year-old life had come and gone in a flash.

Walking the few blocks to my Capitol Hill home after the concert, I heard lots of people whistling the tune they had just learned. They were happy…and that made me happy. That's why I whistle.

A Whistle That Touches My Heart

Name: Father Michael Sliney, LC
Home: Rye, NY
Job: Catholic priest, spiritual director
Fr. Michael's *Whistle*: Communications skills
How I Know Fr. Michael: For several years, my son Justus was in a youth leadership program run by Fr. Michael.

***Whistle* in Action**: If Ronald Reagan was the "Great Communicator" of politics, then Father Michael Sliney is the "Great Communicator" of eternal truths. Of the 200 e-mails I get daily, my two favorites are from Fr. Michael. One is a thirty-second video commentary on various spiritual and practical subjects, and the other is a quote from a holy or wise person (e.g. Saint Therese of Lisieux or C. S. Lewis) with a few sentences of reflection by Fr. Michael, whose ministry is to help strengthen the faith of Catholics. Through his compelling and actionable communications, Fr. Michael has helped me better realize that faith is not a one-and-done thing. Sunday church is important, but understanding one's faith and practicing it with conviction and joy is an everyday journey. As Fr. Michael opines on humility, sin, forgiveness, and love, his selfie videos typically feature the hubbub of New York City in the background. It's a fitting metaphor for the task at hand: how to be *in* the world but not *of* the world, to have one's vision planted on the divine and eternity, though we have feet of clay. With this simple gift, Fr. Michael is touching many hearts and souls, and I am blessed to be among them.

CHAPTER 17
Happy Birthday, Carole

THE FIRST RULE of a successful marriage is: keep the wife happy.

The second rule is: keep the mother-in-law happy.

The third rule: it's hard to make everyone happy.

Vacations have always presented a challenge for delivering timely birthday serenades. My regimen is disrupted. I don't look at my calendar as much or even wear a watch every day. Heck, when we're at Lost Valley Ranch in remote Colorado (a dude ranch we go to every August), my phone doesn't even work, so I rely on a rickety landline in the lobby of the lodge. Disconnecting is the point of vacation, but birthday serenade duty calls, remote destinations notwithstanding.

There we were, in South Dakota, communing with bison, touring mountain carvings (Crazy Horse Memorial and Mount Rushmore), and getting away from the East Coast rat race.

It was August 18, my mother-in-law's birthday, which was duly noted in my calendar. Early in the day, my wife and children called Carole and wished her a happy birthday. Where I was at that crucial moment is still a matter of debate, but what is clear is that August 19 arrived, and for the first time since knowing Carole (fifteen years at that point), I hadn't whistled on her actual birthday.

The morning of August 19, my wife's cell phone rang, and tears and sobs greeted her. A string of concerns spilled into my wife's ear: *Chris didn't whistle; he mustn't care anymore; he doesn't love me; he whistles for all my friends but not for me; what have I done to deserve this…tell me!*

Thank God my wife didn't just hand the phone to me. She hung up and looked at me with a mixture of *how could you, poor thing,* and *oh boy, let's see how you handle this one.*

Because of my day job, I've grown adept at handling upset bigwig politicians and annoyed billionaire businessmen, but this was a problem in a different galaxy, and would require a very thoughtful and sophisticated response.

Complete and total capitulation: there would be no explanation, just a sword upon which I would swiftly fall.

Not wanting to drag out the pain, I called Carole right away. On the spot, I came up with a creative solution. I offered to whistle "Happy Birthday" twice, effectively a penalty or a bonus, depending on your perspective. That, plus professions of love and regret, seemed to help. Despite the sword's swift and deep penetration, it wasn't as bad as I thought.

Then again, I've never made that mistake a second time. Forever more, August 18 will be a day that Rule #2 and Rule #1 switch: keep Mother-in-Law Carole happy.

CHAPTER 18

Who Really Shut the Government Down?

THERE'S A CLASSIC LINE from the 1976 Lynyrd Skynyrd album *One More from the Road*, where band leader Ronnie Van Zant says to the audience: "What song is it you want to hear?" He already knew the answer, clearly asking the question to tease and get them even more fired up.

"Freebird!" came the answer in unison from the then insane audience.

The rest is history, as the band proceeded to knock out a gigantic, fourteen-minute version of their signature song, which still warms the hearts of classic rock fans.

Nineteen years later, in December of 1995, on a cold day in Washington, DC, it was hot inside an ornate room in the U.S. Capitol. An epic budget battle was coming to a head, and my lips were soon to be at the center of it. That's when I channeled Ronnie Van Zandt, asking the second most powerful member of the U.S. House of Representatives, "What song do you want to hear?" In this case, I had no idea what the answer was going to be.

How I even ended up in that room, filled with the top Republican leaders in Congress, less than a year after getting the boot from another congressman's office is a testament to how unpredictable life is and how misfortune can be our friend.

Before becoming spokesman for the U.S. House Budget Committee (the position that brought me to that ornate room), I worked for U.S. Representative Rod Grams, a Republican from Minnesota, as his press secretary. My departure from his employment was bizarre. A few days after he was elected to the U.S. Senate, in November 1994, his chief of staff, Chris Erikstrup, led me deep into a warren of dimly lit storage rooms in a congressional office building and summarily fired me. "The Congressman no longer needs your services," she informed me. No explanation. That was it. I was out the door within the hour. It smacked of Kremlin intrigue, minus the bullet.

There were several reasons that job didn't work out—particularly differing communications philosophies—but I was to blame as well.

In April of that year, 1994, I won the international whistling competition. There was an overwhelming rush of media attention. I did dozens of radio interviews and TV appearances, including *The Tonight Show with Jay Leno* and the *Today Show with Katie Couric*. It was exciting and heady. In retrospect, I didn't balance it properly with my day job. Getting the boot from a job taught me some good lessons.

In the meantime, though, I needed a job. Within minutes of getting my walking papers, I was on the phone with a good friend. "Marie, it's Chris Ullman. Greetings."

Marie Wheat was a policy analyst on the Republican staff of the House Budget Committee. No time for chitchat, I launched into my pitch: Republicans had just taken over Congress for the first time in forty years, so the Budget Committee's Republican "minority" staff would be adding bodies as it moved to "majority" status; I had just been fired from my job ("Good riddance," she said, knowing how I felt about them). Simply put, they needed a spokesman and I needed a job!

Marie said they hadn't even started thinking about hiring a PR person, so the timing was perfect. I hand-delivered my resume (no e-mail in 1994), hopefully getting a head start on the competition, and then emptied out my desk.

Navigating the fact that I had been booted, versus having left of my own volition, wasn't as bad as I feared. Thankfully, Marie had known me for several years (we had previously worked together at a free-market advocacy group called Citizens for a Sound Economy), so I had a friend on the inside. Also, people change jobs on Capitol Hill as often as they brush their teeth, so people shrugged it off that it didn't work out.

Within three weeks I had the job…head of Communications for the U.S. House Budget Committee, under the leadership of Chairman John R. Kasich, (R-OH). I was quite blessed as it was a heady time to work on Capitol Hill. I was there on the steps of the U.S. Capitol when Speaker Newt Gingrich introduced the Contract with America. History was happening before my eyes, and it was an honor to be a small part of it.

Chastened from my recent experience, I was determined to better balance my whistling with my day job. That goal was going well for a year or so, until a *Washington Post* reporter wanted to write a story on me as I prepared for the 1996 whistling competition. I declined, not wanting to alienate the big boss, Chairman Kasich.

That was painful. Declining a likely positive story in a prominent newspaper is anathema to every fiber of a PR person's body. But, despite the good it could do for my whistling reputation, there were other factors to consider, such as having a job and an income.

The reporter persisted. His reputation as a trustworthy straight-shooter was compelling, and got me to revisit his request. Then he said he had a brilliant solution, and asked me to trust him. I eventually got buy-in from Chairman Kasich's personal press secretary and my immediate boss, then proceeded with lips pursed and fingers crossed.

There's an old expression among politicians: "Doesn't matter what they say about me as long as they spell my name right." With that guiding principle, the reporter, Guy Gugliotta, proceeded to write a remarkably witty and creative article.

Not only did he spell my boss' name right, he included it eighteen times…in CAPS! That's right, in almost every sentence of the article were the words "JOHN R. KASICH." However obvious the conceit, he did it seamlessly, the mark of a truly talented writer.

I rushed to get the paper that morning. A few sentences in, I realized Gugliotta's approach and laughed out loud. Appropriately paranoid, though, I asked my housemates what they thought and talked to a few friends on the Hill that morning before seeing what the senior people on the Budget Committee thought.

Some of my favorite lines:

> Up to now, Chris Ullman has maintained a scrupulously low profile as JOHN R. KASICH's tireless promoter, but very soon he will once again risk all. Ullman, a tall, dapper bachelor with a Republican haircut and an affinity for bow ties, learned to whistle in Massapequa Park, N.Y., when he was 5, long before he knew JOHN R. KASICH. Ullman, like JOHN R. KASICH, is gifted with a large mouth, and can cover 2 1/2 octaves when he's in shape. *People magazine* wrote him up, and he jammed on the "Today" and "Tonight" shows, a double-whammy never achieved by either Grams or JOHN R. KASICH. Late last year, basking in JOHN R. KASICH's reflected glory, Ullman appeared on "Equal Time," where he whistled the William Tell Overture and "In the Mood," wowing Dee Dee Myers and Mary Matalin, who remarked that "this may be the coolest show of all time."

Thank the dear Lord, it was an instant hit. Chairman Kasich, who was then cultivating a hip public image, was pleased with being featured in an article about a fun and quirky staffer, and I got some great ink on my whistling. The article helped cement my reputation on Capitol Hill as *The Whistler*. Unlike my time in Rep. Grams' office, though, I had figured out how to balance the whistling with my day job, which I've been able to sustain for the past twenty-one years.

Back to that ornate room in the U.S. Capitol and the big budget battle.

Just steps from the Speaker's office, top Republican leaders were debating whether to make peace or keep fighting with President Clinton. It was a gigantic budget show-down, and someone was going to blink.

Passions were high and tempers flared. At stake was the impact of a government shutdown and who would get the blame.

The biggest wigs in Congress debated and duked it out: would principle or pragmatism prevail? It was amazing to even be in the room where it was happening. That's one of the greatest perks of being a PR person. We often get to tag along with the boss, riding the slipstream of power, becoming silent witnesses to history. And a historic time it was. Decades later, Republicans are still smarting over the decisions made that day.

After an hour or so of back and forth, with no resolution in sight, the number two House Republican, Majority Leader Dick Armey, a gravelly-voiced Texan with a splendid slow drawl, took the floor. Every head turned towards him. He pointed across the room and issued a simple command: "You...whistle for us."

Every head then swung toward me. It was like a tennis match.

This was cognitive dissonance at its best. One moment I was minding my own business, pondering the PR implications of shutting down the government, and the next I was the unexpected center of attention, and not for budgetary reasons.

Instinctively, I turned around, as if the person he was pointing to was behind me. But there was only a wall.

"No, you with the bow tie, whistle for us."

The room was silent. A hundred pair of eyes set upon me.

Puncturing the quiet, Chairman John Kasich, piped up, saying, "Hey, he's my press secretary." A rare reversal of whose caboose is hooked to whose engine.

"What song do you want to hear?" I asked.

"'Dixie,'" responded the majority leader.

Uh-oh. "Dixie" was problematic. When asked to whistle that in the past, I'd sometimes veered into "The Yellow Rose of Texas," which has a similar structure and tune. Now, with no time to ponder or rehearse, I had one chance to get it right.

I retreated into myself, pushing aside the commotion and pressure. With my eyes closed, I searched my brain for the words to the song, which I knew would bring the right tune to my lips. From some recess of grey matter they appeared, scrolling like a news ticker in New York's Times Square. "I wish I was in the land of cotton...Old times there are not forgotten…Look away! Look away! Look away! Dixie Land."

It was only a second or two, but seemed like an eternity. I reminded myself that the passage of time seems different depending on whether you are on stage or in the audience.

My whistle filled the room. Suddenly, I'd gone from silent observer to accidental entertainer. Even after hundreds of command performances over the years at parties, in the halls at work, and at 1000-person conferences, I still find it to awkward to go from zero to sixty in just seconds. I'm not a prima-donna, demanding a dressing room stocked with green M&Ms, but there are benefits to warming up and getting psyched before a performance. Usually all I request is a glass of ice water. I also have a no-kissing policy for twenty-four hours before a performance. Kissing makes my lips mushy and mushy lips are bad for whistlers. I wasn't married or dating anyone at that time so that wasn't a problem at this impromptu gig.

All that said, I have gotten used to jumping into the fray on a moment's notice, though I sometimes lament that Luciano Pavarotti was *never* asked to perform a little Puccini at a cocktail party or on a street corner. But then I remember I'm not Luciano Pavarotti, one of the greatest operatic tenors of all time.

I resisted my inclination to whistle with eyes closed; what I saw amazed me. Senior elected officials' heads bobbed, smiles as big as the Capitol dome ringed the room. Fellow staffers who knew of my whistling seemed to take it in stride, while first-timers tried to make sense of what they were experiencing.

I suspect there was a whole lot of cognitive dissonance gripping the grand ornate room: *top elected officials...serious budget debate...impending government shutdown...the future of the Republican Party...bowtie wearing staffer whistling "Dixie"...laughter...smiles...applause.*

Of course. Makes perfect sense. (Maybe in a Monty Python movie.)

Feeling high from the experience, I was tempted to go into concert mode and start jamming, letting loose some of my whistling tricks and flourishes. Halfway through, though, I concluded that this was probably meant as comic relief, so less was better.

I brought the piece in for a landing after one time through (main verse and refrain) plus a repeat of the refrain, "Look away, look away, look away Dixieland," slower with a warbled last note.

For a moment, there was silence as the last notes resonated in the grand room. Then it came...an eruption of applause. Relief, then shock washed over me as a flurry of handshakes and pats on the back greeted me.

The meeting that would effectively decide whether to shut down the federal government summarily ended, and everyone filed out of the room.

But there was no decision...or was there?

Capitol Hill police officers standing guard outside had quizzical looks on their faces, wondering what had just happened.

I left the Capitol through the tunnel connecting it to the House side and returned to my office. It seemed like a dream, but it was as real as the government shutdown that happened a day later.

I guess there was a decision. Dick Armey wanted to fight, and I unwittingly provided the battle cry. News stories never mentioned my role...I was the stealth whistler.

A *Whistle* That Touches My Heart

Name: Daniel Akerson
Home: McLean, VA
Job: Former Chairman and CEO of General Motors; former Head of Global Buyout at The Carlyle Group.
Dan's *Whistle*: Moral compass
How I Know Dan: Dan and I met in 2003 when he became a colleague at The Carlyle Group.

***Whistle* in Action**: In my thirty-year career I've never met anyone like Dan Akerson. He's whip smart, refreshingly blunt, and brimming with opinions as forceful as his ethical backbone is strong. A U.S. Naval Academy grad who served on a destroyer, Dan took his engineering degree and turned it into a business career that defines the American dream, culminating at the helm of General Motors, the iconic global company. Soon after meeting in 2003, I discovered beneath the executive exterior a man of deep faith, dry wit, ready charity, and a North Star of ethical probity that burns brightly. Anyone who thinks corporate America is ethically challenged would find comfort in Dan Akerson. Dan's not a chat-about-the-weather kind of guy. In our many conversations over the years I picked his brain about weighty subjects past and present, with an emphasis on discerning what is the right thing to do. In a world where the gravitational pull is toward expediency, having a moral compass that puts justice ahead of convenience is inspiring. While I consider myself an upstanding guy, having a friend of Dan's stature preach a gospel of ethics has helped strengthen my backbone in matters small and large and will be a star that lights my path for years to come.

CHAPTER 19
Happy Birthday, Uncle Terry

"DADDY, WHISTLING SAVES LIVES," exclaimed my eleven year-old daughter.

I thought I had heard it all. Whistling is delightful. Whistling is annoying. It gives you lip wrinkles. It's bad to do in newsrooms and a sign of confidence around graveyards. Dogs howl when they hear screechy high notes.

But save lives? I don't think so.

My daughter Alydia started whistling when she was five. The summer of 2006, she declared that she would teach herself how to whistle, and she succeeded. Meanwhile, her younger siblings then and since have shown little interest.

With her newfound ability in hand, talk of her competing in the whistling competition crept into family conversations periodically.

"Someday," we said. No pressure, though.

Then I was asked to judge the 2013 international competition, which would take place in Louisburg, NC, the longtime home of the competition. I had judged it once before and thoroughly enjoyed it. I had hoped it would be less stressful than competing, but it wasn't. Judging is quite difficult, staying focused, suppressing biases, being sensitive and perceptive hour after hour. With a keen sense of duty to the whistling community, I agreed to do it.

As the deadline for registering to compete got closer, Alydia decided she would join me as an observer at the convention. This way she could scope out the competition and see how talented she really was. Good move.

A few days before we headed south to Louisburg, my wife's friend Suzanne asked if I could whistle "Happy Birthday" for her Uncle Terry, who was gravely ill in the hospital and about to enter hospice. I noted his name, number, and the date on my calendar, which happened to be the main day of the upcoming whistling competition.

That day soon arrived. During the lunch break in the competition, Alydia and I and two fellow judges, both former whistling champions, jumped in my car and went to a burger joint just down the road from the competition venue. After we ate, before I got back in the car, I called Uncle Terry and whistled "Happy Birthday" for him.

It turned out he loved whistling, and his niece Suzanne thought it would boost his spirits on his birthday. He and I chatted for a moment, and then I asked if I could call him back. I got in the car with my fellow former champions—Greg Nye Smith and Mimi Drummond—and asked if they'd be willing to whistle a song for Uncle Terry. They agreed, and we quickly settled upon "Don't Sit under the Apple Tree."

I called Uncle Terry back, introduced everyone, and then without any rehearsal, we launched into a swing-version of the song, made famous by Glenn Miller. (I once whistled that song with the Glenn Miller Orchestra, but that's another story.) It was a sweet and joyous moment.

Our judgeships were calling, so after some brief chitchat, we wished him well and said goodbye.

For better or worse, my ability to segment and stay focused kicked in, and I didn't think about Uncle Terry again until a few weeks later, when my wife gave Alydia and me shocking news. Uncle Terry was out of the hospital, but hadn't entered hospice.

"Did he pass away?" I asked.

"No, he's getting better!"

"What?!"

That's when Alydia declared the curative powers of whistling.

I've long thought that making time to touch a lonely, sad, or suffering soul, whether through a happy tune or a needed hug, can be a powerful elixir. But save lives? Who knew?

The start of Chris' whistling journey: a powerful pucker even at age 5.

No, that's not a perm…Chris at age 15 in 1978…when he wasn't riding his Schwinn Stingray, he was skateboarding.

Betty Buchanan, conductor of the Capitol Hill Choral Society, taught Chris how to turn notes into music.

Elizabeth Foster's support created the foundation for Chris' success as a whistler.

Chris whistles a happy tune for his bride Kristen at their wedding in 2001.

Chris with Allen De Hart, who organized the whistling convention for 40 years. Allen passed away in 2016 at 90 years young.

*Katie Couric puckers with Chris and his blues band after
an appearance on the* Today Show *in 1994.*

Chris jammed with the band on The Tonight Show *with
Jay Leno after winning his first championship in 1994.*

*Chris and his mom Fran after winning his fourth and
final grand championship in 2000.*

From 1993–2000, Chris and Tanguay Desgagne were the reigning whistling grand champions, each winning four times.

Chris and Senator John Ashcroft, who share the same birthday, perform at a Christmas party in 2000.

At a gig in the Oval Office, President George W. Bush likes what he hears.

President Bush thanks Chris for his private Oval Office concert. Chris holds a "review" of the gig that the president wrote for Chris' father "Bub."

Chris and his boss Mitch Daniels perform "Dueling Banjos" for the president.

*Chris whistles "Yankee Doodle" at the top of the Washington Monument
during its repair following an earthquake.
Photo Credit: Tami Heilemann*

*Chris challenges the audience to "find your whistle" at TEDx Mid-Atlantic in 2013.
Photo Credit: Richard A. Bloom*

Chris performs the national anthem at Duke's Cameron Indoor Stadium in 2015.
Photo Credit: Jon Gardiner/Duke Photography

Chris and his friend Preston Ulman take turns whistling for each other.

CHAPTER 20
Hi TED, My Name Is CHRIS

ON STAGE, David Rubenstein was delivering his first TEDx talk, on the importance of philanthropy. Backstage was Colin Powell, next up in the queue. At fifteen minutes per speech, the TED emphasis on impact and brevity meant David wouldn't be long.

Colin Powell, as in General Colin Powell of military and diplomatic fame, was about to talk about leadership in times of adversity. It would have been nice to meet him and thank him for his service, but I decided not to upset his pre-talk mojo.

Applause signaled the end, and from behind a curtain came David walking briskly, almost bumping into Powell. Their acquaintanceship goes back many years, so they shook hands and chatted for thirty seconds.

I've always wondered if famous people get excited when they see other famous people. Neither of them seemed too excited.

Sarge Salman, one of the event organizers, started to escort David and me out of the building. Within seconds, though, David was on his Blackberry and already five feet ahead.

As is common after a Rubenstein speech, the organizers gushed with praise and appreciation. This time, I was the recipient on David's behalf. Then Sarge said they were planning next year's TEDx Mid-Atlantic, and asked if I knew of any interesting speakers.

Ever vigilant for an opportunity to whistle at a high-profile event, but hesitant to get bogged down in a whistling discussion while I was trying to catch up with the boss, I handed Sarge my day job business card and simply said, "Look me up."

We shook hands and I didn't think about it again.

Five months later, the phone rang in my office.

"Hi, this is Chris Ullman."

"I cannot f**king believe that you didn't tell me. You are a g-ddamn champion whistler?! This is unbelievable. Why didn't you tell me?"

"Who is this?"

"It's Sarge Salman, from TEDx Mid-Atlantic."

The light went on in my brain as I recalled handing Sarge my card with no explanation backstage at Sydney Harmon Hall in Penn Quarter of Washington, DC.

I doubt Sarge was the first to curse because of my whistling. All the others I've driven crazy over the years just did it under their breath or behind my back.

Sarge said he liked the idea of me doing a TEDx whistle-talk, as speakers do more than talk at these events, but we'd have to figure out what my message would be.

Utterly pumped at the prospect of doing a TEDx talk, I hung up the phone and was instantly filled with dread. What would I say? Why would anyone care? Memorize a fifteen minute presentation word-for-word? Totally nuts and totally exhilarating.

TED talks have become quite the rage over the past ten to fifteen years. TED stands for Technology, Entertainment, and Design. They were started by Richard Saul Wurman in 1984, with a simple mantra of "ideas worth spreading." For those not familiar with TED, my definition is thoughtful people talking about innovative ideas in short blocks of time, usually fifteen minutes. At a typical TED or TEDx conference, there are a few dozen speakers over a one- or two-day period in front of a live audience. At the TEDx I spoke at, there were around 750 people.

What a great opportunity. Pay a small fee to sit for two days and listen to smart and thought-provoking people talk about topics far and wide. TED became so popular it spawned the TEDx, independently-organized regional versions under the auspices of TED.

One of my favorite TED talks is of a Stanford professor who helped create the "captcha," which is the funky code you have to interpret and type in when buying concert tickets online. In it, he talks about a second-generation captcha that is helping to digitize all the world's books. Amazing! From captcha to whistling, that's TED.

The bar was high, so I began a seven-month journey of pondering and practicing.

The creative process fascinates me. Where do great ideas come from? Do they just emerge from thin air, or are they the result of a structured process that fosters and guides out-of-the-box thinking? Sure, provocative and compelling ideas can just pop into your head, but I've found that to be a consistently creative person, you need to harness the other side of the brain. For me, that means gathering information from disparate sources, bouncing ideas off lots of smart people, truly understanding the objective, being open to new things, and understanding human nature. It's a puzzle, a custom jigsaw puzzle, one that's not necessarily rectangular.

As I thought about my talk, I knew the main ingredients would be whistling and storytelling. But what else? What spices would make it a savory stew? How about a piano accompanist? Yum.

One day while out for a bike ride, I was thinking about my talk, and the prospect of having a violinist do a duet with me just popped in my head. Yeah, that would be different. A whistler and a violist doing "Dueling Banjos," the iconic song from the 1972 film *Deliverance*.

Now we'd got quite a meal, but the main flavor was still missing. Cajun? Italian? Indian?

What's the point? I asked myself over and over.

I tried to picture the event being over and a CNN reporter interviewing people as they filed out of the hall just having heard the whistler. What would they say to the reporter when asked what I had just said? What did I *want* them to say?

It just wasn't coming to me, so I focused on the parts I could control: coming up with my best whistling stories and finding the pianist and violinist. Sifting through whistling stories was easy. Finding a violinist who could improvise well was hard, until I walked into David Rubenstein's office and asked for his help.

On the spot, he speed-dialed the music director of the National Symphony Orchestra (it helps to be the chairman of the John F. Kennedy Center for the Performing Arts, home of the National Symphony), got her on the phone, introduced me, and then left the room. Within five minutes, I had my man. The NSO had a seasoned violinist, Glenn Donnellan, who was also an accomplished fiddle player, fully capable of jamming and improvisation.

Selecting an accompanist was an easy choice. Glenn Pearson, who'd saved me when David asked me to whistle at Carlyle's big investor conference in 2015, loved the idea of doing a TEDx together.

I started writing a script, rehearsing with Glenn and Glenn, and going on more bike rides, hoping inspiration would strike again. Like a sunrise that illuminates incrementally, the central message revealed itself over time.

I hadn't cured cancer, or climbed Mount Everest blind, or invented a high-tech widget that changed the world. Nope. I'm just a whistler. That was it—*just* a whistler. Finally, the theme was revealed.

My tale was a simple one, presenting a common skill in unusual ways, touching people's hearts and tickling their funny bones. I inject joy and humanity into otherwise serious situations. I'd taken my simple gift and performed for presidents, serenaded hundreds of people on their birthdays, and become friends with a young man who couldn't speak, but could whistle.

I had found my *whistle*. My *whistle* was literally a whistle. But everyone, I concluded, had a *whistle*, a gift that could be shared with people around them, making the world a little better, a little sweeter, one person at a time. Just as I had found my *whistle*, I would charge the audience with finding their *whistles*.

The meal was complete. Now I had to fine-tune and memorize my talk, a terrifying prospect for someone with a less than stellar memory.

I decided to practice on my children. At first, I simply read it to them, and then moved "off-book" as I committed it to memory. That was the hard part. Time after time, my children said, "Daddy, you said it different last time." Their candor was invaluable. I wish more adults were similarly honest and constructive.

Obsession took over. I practiced in the car, at home, at work. I worked harder on this talk than any presentation I'd ever done. I watched lots of TED talks to get tips on what made them effective. I even watched a TED talk on how to give a TED talk! I rehearsed several times with my accompanists.

This was gonna be a hoot! But I was still worried. There's a line from a Billy Joel song: "Get it right the first time, that's the main thing. Get it right the next, that's not the same thing." I had one chance to bring all the parts together and get it right. "Right" meant several things: I had to educate, entertain, and inspire the audience; show them what whistling can be; fill them with joy and laughter; and get them to think about finding, developing, and sharing their *whistle*. A heavy lift, but doable.

The Glenns and I were the last talk in the morning session. Done with my energy-expelling pacing and a dose of prayer, Glenn Pearson and I took our positions on stage, and the first notes of "Take the 'A' Train" jumped from the baby grand piano and flowed from my lips. It was the start of a tapestry of songs and stories, from my childhood paper route to the Oval Office, through the hearts of a banker and a birthday girl and a handicapped boy, propelled by rollicking piano and sassy fiddle and soaring whistle.

My final song was "The Battle Hymn of the Republic," which I had performed for President Bush in the Oval Office. With the last note still resonating in the performance hall, the audience rose to its feet, shocking me. I was gratified and humbled beyond all expectations. My final words were, "Now go find your whistle."

I walked off the stage, let out a primal scream, and high-fived Sarge, who up to the last minute was probably wondering if having a whistler do a TEDx talk was a good idea or not.

Among my many unusual whistling experiences, my TEDx talk ranks near the top. It was as deeply satisfying as it was challenging and nerve-wracking. The best part was that I was able to get my message of *find your whistle* to a larger audience, just as I hope this book will do.

A *Whistle* That Touches My Heart

Name: John Stark
Home: Chevy Chase, MD
Job: Securities lawyer, cyber-security consultant
John's *Whistle*: Enthusiastic creativity
How I Know John: We met at the U.S. Securities and Exchange Commission in 1997 when John was an attorney and I ran the office of public affairs.

Whistle **in Action**: Have a notepad ready any time you talk with John Stark, because you'll come away with several new ideas. Give John raw materials, and he will create innovative finished products. Present a challenge, and he will come up with solutions you hadn't thought of. Throw a road block in his way, and he'll leap over it. Give him a ream of blank paper, and he'll write a book. I first witnessed this enthusiastic creativity in 1997, when John combined his knowledge of the law with a computer and used it to fight securities fraud on the Internet, a first for the U.S. government. In the twenty years since, he's continued to turn ideas into reality, forming his own cyber-security consulting firm and writing a book on how to protect against cyber thieves. I love to spend time with John. No matter what issue I'm wrestling with, personal, professional, or artistic, John has thoughtful and actionable ideas to help tackle a challenge or turn a germ of an idea into something tangible and exciting. Whether it's simply watching him in action or being the beneficiary of his enthusiastic creativity, John has touched my heart and my life in meaningful ways.

CHAPTER 21
The General and the Hymn

THE IWO JIMA MEMORIAL on the grounds of Arlington National Cemetery is a holy place to Marines and their families. Joe Rosenthal's Pulitzer Prize-winning photograph of Marines raising Old Glory atop Mt. Suribachi during World War II enshrined in copper is one of the most iconic memorials in Washington.

On a sunny and warm weekday morning in the spring of 2015, I stood beside the memorial. Two feet in front of me, Marine Corps Major General Michael Regner stood at attention, hands by his side, staring into my eyes, his face a rock of seriousness.

I had been looking forward to this day for two months. David Rubenstein was set to announce publicly that he was donating $5.37 million to refurbish the statue and surrounding public spaces. It was another in his long line of patriotic philanthropy gifts in support of institutions and documents of public significance.

Before a throng of reporters and TV cameras, David told how his father enlisted in the Marines in World War II and why this memorial was so special to him. Jonathan Jarvis, head of the National Park Service (which maintains the memorial), and Major General Regner spoke of how David's gift would return this majestic memorial to its former luster and add needed modern amenities, like bathrooms and educational resources.

After all the hubbub, I chatted with the general for a few minutes. He was warm and engaging. Standing beside the august memorial, feeling inspired, I asked the general if I could whistle "The Marines' Hymn" for him. I wasn't sure how he would react, him being a bigwig general.

Without hesitation, he immediately stood at attention and waited for my delivery, as if a switch had been flipped in him. Like the memorial beside us, the hymn was sacred as well. I had never witnessed, let alone experienced, such a visceral patriotic reaction in someone. This man so loves his country and his Corps that the only response to a whistler offering to perform "The Marines' Hymn" was total attention. I was and remain awed.

The pressure rising, I wanted to make sure I didn't whistle "The Army Goes Rolling Along" by accident, the kind of mistake I could make. So I locked on the words: "From the halls of Montezuma, to the shores of Tripoli," which triggered the tune in my head. We were standing so close to each other, I thought I should step back as I prepared to whistle, but he seemed fine with it, focused solely on respecting the hymn, so I stayed where I was.

I started to whistle. He didn't budge. He didn't smile. He stood at full attention as the notes and unspoken words fell upon his ears. He stared into my eyes. I couldn't look away. I was arranging the piece in real time, trying to be respectful and compelling.

That latter objective likely didn't matter to him. It's not about being entertained, it's about duty, honor, country. The hymn is a way to honor the Corps and all its brave men and women have accomplished and sacrificed for 241 years.

I finished whistling and he shook my hand. Only then did he smile.

We exited our private little bubble. There was no audience, it was just the two of us in a remarkable mind meld. I consider myself patriotic, but I was in the presence of a patriot. I learned a lot that day, hearing the words of a major general who has led troops into battle, risking life and limb to protect us and our freedoms, and seeing how his wordless demeanor during the hymn spoke volumes about what the Corps and his country mean to him.

CHAPTER 22

Happy Birthday, Alexandra

EVERY DAY, I PRAY that the Lord will make me his humble and grateful servant, doing His will and not mine. We'll leave it to Him for my over-all score, but among the many times I've fallen flat, here's one time that I blew the top off the humil-o-meter.

I called Alexandra, the wife of a friend, on her birthday. This was probably the second or third time I had serenaded her. A landmark birthday got her on the list in the first place. She answered the phone, so we chatted for a moment before launching into the whistle. The call ended seconds after I finished whistling.

It was a weird call. I felt like she was bored and didn't appreciate my reaching out. That was odd. In fact, I couldn't recall that having happened before. So, I did what any self-respecting champion whistler would do: I deleted her from the birthday serenade list.

Then and there, a summary dismissal.

There was even some dark joy as I pressed delete; *the Whistler* should not be messed with.

Only appreciative subjects would receive THE "HAPPY BIRTHDAY" WHISTLE.

Then I proceeded with my busy and important life.

Then I got a phone call from her husband telling me how much she loved it.

Then I gulped and put her back on the list.

Then I had to figure out how to grow back to my original six-foot height, having been taken down several pegs.

I'm still working on it.

CHAPTER 23

Communing with the Kings

AS I SPOKE TO THE WAITRESS, the words formed perfectly in my brain, but sounded odd as they exited my mouth. Not slurred, but a little fuzzy and slow.

I took a sip of water, and it didn't all go where intended.

It was around six in the evening in mid-April 1996. I sat alone at a table at Corky's Ribs & BBQ in Memphis, just having driven five hours with the top down in my red Miata roadster, all the while whistling, on the heels of three previous days of whistling more than five hours a day. There were two more days to go, for a full thirty hours—more than half a work week—whistling.

If you had asked me before I'd embarked on this week-long circumnavigation of Tennessee if it were possible to whistle for five hours straight every day for a week, I would have said no, emphatically. Not possible. Not desirable. Banish the thought.

Heck, who could tolerate that much uninterrupted whistling? Even I couldn't bear that much puckering and blowing, the high-pitched notes and the repetition. Hearing the same pieces and phrases over and over and over, it's enough to drive a person crazy.

Ostensibly, my Graceland pilgrimage was about communing with the King, but Elvis and his tiger-patterned living room were actually a beacon that I'd pointed myself toward on my quest to reclaim the whistling crown, lost the year before. It was the trifecta of multi-tasking adventures: Graceland pilgrimage + extended Miata top-down time + intense rehearsing.

I had owned my car for six years at that point. Mr. Miata, as he was known, was means and metaphor. Whether it was top-downing on the New Jersey Turnpike heading to New York City to see friends, or cruising through the Smoky Mountains of Tennessee to seek Elvis, it enabled me to check in with the sun and wind and check out from the rat race of the day job and hectic pace of my DC life.

The idea to commune with Elvis had been rumbling around in my head for several years. Then opportunity and purpose collided in the winter of 1996. Still stinging from having come in second place at the 1995 whistling competition, I did a lot of soul searching about how to step up my game.

As a lifelong fan of classical music, I was familiar with the tales of intense focus and grueling rehearsal schedules that top musicians keep to achieve and maintain that greatness. Since I've never been a full-time musician, I've always scrambled to shoehorn in as much practice time as possible. My daily work commute by car became a core tool for putting in the time. That was at least an hour a day, plus another thirty minutes at home, along with whatever pucker time I could get in while walking places. I'd found that it was a daily process of piecing together quality and quantity to produce excellence over time. So, maybe a serious solo trip to Graceland would get me the time I needed to perfect my songs and techniques.

Lips are muscles. To keep them limber yet strong requires tons of flexing, i.e. puckering. A pucker, however nice and necessary it is for kissing, is not a natural position for one's lips.

Try it, right now. Slowly form a pucker. You'll see how many muscles are involved in elongating the lips and forming them into a tight circle. Look in the mirror while you're doing it. For a few moments, it's easy. But try holding it for one minute straight. It becomes surprisingly tiring. See, I told you.

What you're doing is testing and developing your embouchure. It's a neat French word that means both the conditioning and positioning of your lips, typically in the context of playing a wind instrument. If you've ever played a trombone, flute, trumpet, or oboe, you're nodding right now, and maybe even licking your lips, recalling sweet memories of high school or college band or orchestra. For non-mouth musicians, trust me, it's all about the embouchure.

Because a pucker is so dependent on well-conditioned muscles, the road to an effective embouchure is paved with countless hours of practice. It's like building and maintaining any relationship; sure, quality matters, but time is just as important. There's no substitute for just being with someone, just as whistling a happy tune while walking down the street or up the stairwell or through the garage is priceless.

How tiring could it really be? Well, try this: get a three-pound dumbbell and start doing arm curls. I tried it the other day. The first forty curls were effortless, and then I noticed that this tiny weight seemed to be growing. At one hundred curls, I was starting to breathe a little harder. At 150 curls, I had to tell my arm to extend and contract each time; the effortlessness was gone. At 175, I wasn't sure I could keep going. At 200, my muscles were twitching, and I could barely move my arm. I then promptly tried the experiment on my weaker left arm, and only made it to 175. It too became a twitching mass.

That's what puckering for a long time is like, hence why after five hours of straight whistling, my speech was impaired and I had trouble drinking. But I couldn't have lasted anywhere near five hours if I hadn't been practicing constantly for so many years.

So, that's quantity—but what about quality?

The process of turning notes into music is fascinating. I've long loved learning the notes and then bringing them to life, whether I was singing or whistling. When I give presentations at schools, I show kids how this process works. I whistle "Mary Had a Little Lamb" in its simplest form, note for note, in a staccato, march-like manner, which is how most kids learn and sing it.

Then I run through it again. This time I smooth the notes together, make it a little faster, vary the tempo a bit, bend some notes, throw in a few whirligigs, and soon enough, Mary had a jazzy lamb. Like the national anthem, it's a process of making the piece your own while respecting the composer's intentions. I try to make things inviting and fun without being too radical.

Larry Holdridge and Betty Buchanan, gently dispositioned and remarkably talented conductors who led the choirs I was in in high school and then after college, taught me how to turn notes into music. They showed me how thoughtful phrasing brings notes to life and makes a point, just as words flow into sentences, which become paragraphs and chapters. They gave me a solid foundation that I have worked to build upon for more than thirty years. Because of them, I try to build beautiful things with my musical toolbox.

For example, on my CD, *The Symphonic Whistler*, I perform a delightful trumpet concerto by Johann Nepomuk Hummel, the greatest pianist of his day and, get this, a pallbearer at Beethoven's funeral.

While rehearsing the piece in preparation for the recording session with a full forty-two piece orchestra, I discovered a section in the third of three movements that sounded better if I slowed the tempo way down. The notes were the same, but injecting a slower tempo into the otherwise fast movement made the piece more distinctive. Such a move might have earned a rebuke from Hummel, but my job was to make the piece mine, interpreted in a way that brought the piece to life and made the greatest use of my instrument and skills.

In addition to getting my lips in the finest form possible, a key goal of the road trip was to settle on the songs that I would perform in the competition, plus a few back-ups in case tie-breakers were needed. I gathered twenty or so songs that were top candidates, packed my small bag (Miata's don't have big trunks), and headed west.

In 1984, I circumnavigated the country on a solo motorcycle coming-of-age journey, catching twenty-eight states, somehow missing Tennessee. It was worth the wait. Emerging from West Virginia into the northeast quadrant of the Volunteer State, the natural beauty and serene wilderness struck me instantly. My spirits rose as I realized that most of this trip was going to be in fifth gear, and with nary a cloud in the sky and the top down.

On the approach to Nashville, I cranked up some great country music—Randy Travis, George Strait, and Clint Black—which made for sweet listening and rehearsing. Unbeknownst to me at the time, a seed was planted, as I would win the 1999 championship with Clint Black's song "This Nightlife," a fast and technically challenging piece with a catchy tune.

I methodically worked my way through the twenty prospective songs. I'd pop in a CD or cassette (remember those?) and whistle it over and over, assessing how well it met the seven criteria that make for a winning performance:

1. Great melody
2. Diversity of tempos and instruments
3. Showcase for my abilities
4. Capacity to be arranged in a memorable way
5. Few to no words
6. Right length (four minutes for popular category and six minutes for classical)
7. Tolerable (could it be whistled incessantly without me going insane?)

Numbers one, three, and four are particularly important.

A great melody is irresistible, but what if you find a real toe-tapper that few people (especially the judges) are familiar with? That's when song selection becomes quite strategic.

Think about the difference between reaction and anticipation. When you listen to one of your favorite songs, so much of the experience and enjoyment is about anticipation. You know what's coming—a favorite lyric or instrument riff, coupled with a tune and tempo that makes your heart stir and spirit sore. That's why we listen to songs over and over. They predictably evoke feelings.

On the other hand, think about what it's like to hear a song for the first time. It's like a first date. You have no idea what's coming. It's all new. You're in reaction mode. Sure, patterns emerge, and if you're astute, you'll quickly pick up on them. Reaction isn't bad, it's just different from anticipation. They're like different sides of the same coin. In fact, reaction is a powerful phenomenon. That's why people love to try new foods, visit strange lands, and date around. There's a thrill in every instance, even if the food is too spicy, the land is filled with mosquitos, and the dates are duds.

What I learned quickly at the whistling competition is that picking the right song is the foundation of a winning performance. Simply put, if you pick a song the judges know ("Ave Maria," Beethoven's Fifth Symphony, or "Clair de Lune"), it has to be the best they've ever heard. If you pick a tune they probably don't know, such as an obscure movement to a Beethoven piano concerto or an upbeat swing song by a no-name country band, they have to like it the first time they hear it.

Each is risky. In the first instance, it's all anticipation. When the emcee announces that Billy Bob is going to perform Beethoven's Fifth, the judges (and everyone in the audience) think, *oh, I know that*. The judges surely know every note. Your rendition has to be simply great— innovative, dynamic, and compelling—and note perfect. What do you add to the piece to make it come alive? There better be something, otherwise people will be bored, and winners are not boring.

On the other hand, perform a piece no one's ever heard of, and you're taking them on that proverbial first date. Your job is to have them tapping their toes and nodding in agreement as you weave fun and lively stories. It can't be a monologue either; they must feel part of the narrative. You welcome them in with your body language and eye contact. The fun must be mutual. The feelings must be positive, immediate, and genuine, like a crush. It's hard to do, but everyone loves the feeling of a crush, even if it's fleeting or even naughty. Then you have them in the palm of your hand.

After having dinner at Corky's, I checked into my hotel, took a nap, and then headed to B.B. King's Blues Club on famous Beale Street in Memphis. I was hoping to see B.B. himself perform, but since I had no problem getting in (it was crowded but not packed), that dream was quickly dashed.

Sweet blues coming from the house band, the King Bees, penetrated my brain and enveloped my body. The pulsating bass and drums reminded me of the rhythms of the road, minus the wind and whistling.

Standing in the back near the bar, nursing a glass of ice water with lime, I had a good vantage point to observe the crowd and band. The crowd voiced its approval with hoots and claps as the set came to an end.

A few moments later, I spied the lead singer standing a few feet from me chatting with someone. As their conversation ended, I made my move. I walked up to him and said, "You guys are great. Do you ever let people sit in with you?"

A silent, perplexed look greeted me. For a few moments, the grizzled old black man pondered the request of the curly-haired young white kid. "What do you play?" he asked skeptically.

Moving in a little closer, over the din of the crowd, I said, "I'm a whistler."

Silence.

Filling the void, I eagerly spit out a few credentials and handed him my business card. It seemed more like an illicit exchange of government secrets than the negotiation of a musical performance.

He was non-committal, nodding slowly, clearly pondering this odd overture. Then he was gone, and I returned to my glass of water and people-watching.

Over the years, I've asked dozens of bands and solo performers if they'd let me sit in with them. I estimate a success rate of around sixty percent—not bad for what is effectively a cold call. Musicians are generally open-minded people who like to mix things up, so while a performing whistler is rare, it's not unheard of. There's a strong incentive for me to do a good job, for everyone's sake.

A few songs into the next set, I started to get tired (I'm not a night owl); the rigors of driving all day in the sun and whistling incessantly were taking their toll. I decided to give it another couple of songs, and then I'd leave.

Then the band leader pulled out a small white card and announced that a guest performer was going to join them. "Looks like we've got a champion whistler in the audience this evening. Will Chris Ullman come on up?"

I heard something that sounded familiar, like sensing my name being spoken while coming out of a deep sleep. Then it clicked. He was calling me! Zig-zagging between people, I zoomed toward the stage. With a few feet still to go, the band let loose the first notes of an upbeat blues tune. In one swift motion, I mounted the stage, put my water down, and took the microphone offered to me by a smiling roadie.

His fingers busy picking out chords and strumming, the leader nodded at me and let a tiny crack of smile shine through, like the first rays of sun that creep over the horizon on a clear summer morning.

I tried to shift quickly from awkward interloper to member of the band in as few notes as possible. The music entered my ears and was absorbed into my brain. The blues have appealed to me since I was a teen: the earthiness, the pining, the thinly veiled joy, and the overt angst of life's latest setback. The rhythms are comforting and fun (jump-boogies, shuffles) and the patterns are logical.

The lead guitarist finished the first verse and jammed for sixteen bars, then the piano took the baton and ran with it for another sixteen bars. The leader caught my eye, and with a slight nod, signaled that I was next.

My heart raced. I licked my lips. With the mic raised and the pianist looking my way, I took the baton and started to run with it. Eyes closed, lipped pursed, notes flowed. I was jamming with the King Bees. I heard a yelp from the audience, and some scattered applause as the presence of a whistler sunk in.

Improvisation is a high wire act. There's no pathway laid out, no prescribed notes to follow. You're not the bass, the rhythm, or the melody, yet you're nestled within them all, wending your way through the stew of sounds. You're connected to the melody and key while exploring alleys and avenues that drive the musical narrative forward, capture the mood, and highlight your instrument and your abilities. It's a fascinating melding of both sides of the brain, structure and creativity in harmony.

Improvisation requires comfort with the unknown. Not knowing what the next note is can be paralyzing. That's why few classical musicians improvise. I grew up listening to classical music, each note dictated by the composer, replete with tempos and stress markings. That helped me with structure. I have Jerry Garcia to thank for the creativity.

Starting around fourteen, I spent countless hours jamming along with Garcia and the Grateful Dead. Through high school, college, and to this day, I am mesmerized by his deeply emotional riffs and meanderings. But Jerry is only one arrow in my improvisational quiver of inspiration. Other favorites are guitarists Carlos Santana, Buddy Guy, Mark Knopfler, B.B. King, Eric Clapton, and the jazz band Spyro Gyra.

As I write these words, I'm jamming with the Jerry Garcia Band on "That's What Love Will Make You Do," an upbeat happy tune. It's such a delight to be a phantom member of the band. It makes my heart soar.

All those years of jamming along with my favorite bands served me well as I jammed with the King Bees.

The crowd, after figuring out what was going on, reacted with delight to my riffs. Each of my turns leading the jam were met with wild applause, yelps, and "Yeah, man." I was startled and inspired by their enthusiasm. Applause is the ultimate approval of the business model. There's not a lot of pondering going on. They either like it or they don't.

Nods of approval and smiles came from the band as well. They were genuinely happy; their flyer on this stranger had paid off.

———————

Mile after mile, three colors dominated my landscape; black, green, and blue, corresponding to asphalt, trees, and sky. It was comforting, rhythmical, like the songs I was auditioning. In addition to managing the reaction/anticipation criterion, I looked for songs that showcased my unique abilities as a whistler (number three on the list above).

Most people are lip whistlers, meaning they pucker and blow. Lip whistling is my mainstay as well. However, I have developed a secret whistling weapon, plus several related techniques that dramatically increase my creative bag o' tricks.

I can whistle with my tongue, which requires no lips. It's a breathier sound with limited highs and lows, which I use as an embellishment to keep my arrangements dynamic. Over the years, I've encountered only a few people who can do it.

I developed this alternative means of whistling as a teenager. Bored one day, I was thinking about the components of a whistle: lips, tongue, and air. What would happen if I took away one of them? I quickly figured out that air is mandatory. First I realized that I can do the lip whistle while my tongue is folded back and out of the way. Then I took away lips, and found that by placing my tongue on the roof of my mouth while continuing to blow, I was able to eke out an anemic whistle. Eureka! I had discovered something hidden within me all these years.

With a bunch more experimentation, I developed two more techniques based on the tongue whistle. One is the 'referee' whistle and the other is the 'wa-wa' whistle. To make the referee whistle, I make the 'brrrrr' sound with my lips, as if I'm cold, while whistling with my tongue. It sounds just like a referee's whistle. The other whistle is formed by saying 'wa-wa' while whistling with my tongue. I sometimes refer to this technique as scat whistling, because it's like improvisational singing by the jazz greats, such as Ella Fitzgerald.

You might be thinking, "Nice, but so what?" I'll tell you, they were huge. Without them, I don't think I would have won four championships.

I quickly realized how this new whistle and its related techniques could be beneficial when arranging a piece of music (number four on the above list). They effectively quadrupled the tools I had in my whistling toolbox. I was like a mechanic whose trusty red Craftsman toolbox was overflowing with wrenches and screwdrivers and ratchets. No longer did I have to rely on one main tool to get the job done.

Arranging music for whistle is fascinating and difficult and liberating. What does "arranging" even mean? It's the process of making the piece mine, meaning figuring out what notes to whistle and techniques to use when adapting a song for the whistle.

"Luck Be a Lady" from the musical *Guys and Dolls* is a great case study. In general, my arranging strategy is to make the songs I whistle delightful and startling. "Delightful" means happy, even funny—it's how I engage the hearts of the audience. "Startling" is about the wow factor ("How'd he do that?!"), engaging the audience's brain. If you can capture their hearts and brains, you've hit the jackpot.

The version of "Luck Be a Lady" I debuted at the 2000 whistling competition and have performed many times since is from an instrumental dance scene, also called "The Crapshooters' Dance." It starts with a dramatic burst of brass and timpani that is repeated two times as it descends the scale. After much tinkering, I came up with an arrangement that enabled me to introduce the lip, referee, and wa-wa whistles in the first five seconds of the song. In the inaugural performance, it caught the audience's hearts and brains right away, as evidenced by the smiles and "Wows!" coming from the rapt audience.

Channeling choir conductors Larry and Betty, I methodically went through the piece section by section, figuring out how to bring the notes to life and truly make it mine. One of the basic things they drilled into us choristers was that repeated phrases should be performed differently. That lesson came in handy, as "Luck Be a Lady" has many repeated sections. For example, at the beginning of the finale, one small phrase is repeated five times in succession. How could I make that interesting and not dreadfully repetitive? I reached into my technique toolbox again and grabbed everything in it! Lip whistle, tongue whistle, referee's whistle, and wa-wa whistle—after trying a score of permutations, I came up with a pattern that was spot-on, driving the musical narrative forward while showcasing my abilities. The audience and judges loved it.

So, this was basically what I did for those thirty hours of top-down whistling. I churned through all of the songs I thought had potential. Some got tossed out because they were too long, others because they were boring or not hard enough or didn't showcase my skills effectively. My march through the twenty candidates yielded pieces for the preliminary and final classical rounds, and a strong piece for the popular preliminary round, but I came up dry on a piece that would wow in the popular finals. More than half way through the trip, and with Graceland nearly in sight, I reached for an album I hadn't even considered, Billy Joel's *Streetlife Serenade*. I popped the CD into the player and listened to the first ten seconds of each song. No, no, no. Great tunes, but they all had words.

Then came the fourth song: "Root Beer Rag," a hyper-fast piano instrumental. I whistled along. Box after box was checked. I soon realized I had a winner, if I could master the complexity. I knew it was doable. A feeling of relief washed over me, though there was much work to so.

The next morning, I arrived at Graceland. What a funky place. The Georgian architecture is grandiose, the animal patterns in the jungle room are kitschy, and the racquetball court out back, now lined with gold and platinum albums, is at odds with recollections of the fat Elvis. Though, as someone who loves racquetball, I found another connection with the King.

I toured the mansion first, which was a tasty appetizer before the garish gravesite entrée. Elvis is flanked by his parents and his paternal grandmother. The whole scene is quite a contrast with the gravesite of

President John F. Kennedy at Arlington National Cemetery, just across the Potomac River from the nation's capital. As a DC resident for so many years, I had been to Kennedy's somber grave many times, so I was startled to see a burial place looking like the aftermath of a Mardi Gras party. Beads, stuffed animals, photographs, posters, cherubs, and other kitsch were in great abundance. Having just witnessed the jungle room in the mansion, I probably shouldn't have been surprised that in death, his final resting place would rival his living large living space.

Standing beside Elvis's grave, I softly whistled "Love Me Tender." It was a fun and respectful few moments. Other fans filed by, paying their respects to the King, either not noticing my gentle serenade or offering knowing smiles.

Though not a huge Elvis fan, I better appreciate his genius having been to his home and seen the fervor of those who worshipped him in life and death. I also whistled a bunch of his songs on the way there to get in the mood. His gospel pieces are my favorite.

Like my mother, I like to take my time in museums and see and read pretty much everything, but the house isn't that big and there isn't all that much to read. Considering how long it took to get there, I spent remarkably little time at the mansion and gravesite, under two hours. That was enough. Ultimately, the house was a rallying point, a reason to get on the road and whistle.

Since my early teens, my philosophy of life has been that happiness is not a destination, but a manner of traveling. One of the more extreme manifestations of this thinking came in 1984. I was in Los Angeles, mid-way through a solo motorcycle trip across America. Despite being just a few miles away from the Pacific Ocean, something I had never seen, I blew it off, telling myself that I came to *see* America, not just *cross* America. What can I say—I was twenty-one and a man on a mission. I knew I'd make it to the Pacific one day; that just wasn't the day.

Pulling out of the Graceland parking lot, I pointed east toward Chattanooga, the third of Tennessee's major cities that I'd visit on my pilgrimage. For another five hours, I intensely whistled "Root Bear Rag,"

Beethoven, and the other selections. There was a little over one week to go to the competition, and it was crunch time.

High in the Appalachian Mountains, a bit west of Chattanooga, I had a moment, maybe an epiphany. The curvy road was smooth and wide; the top was down; the wind was crisp and refreshing; the tunes were cranked; my lips were tired but still firm; the view was alternatingly of vast mountainous green space, then the buildings and homes of Chattanooga in the distance below. It was a liberating moment—the exuberance and great potential of life struck me. It was a great time to be alive, thirty-three years old, healthy, single, free, and living in a great country that prizes travel along great swaths of highway.

Convertibles are metaphorically all about freedom. To be one with nature as countryside whips by is about as good as life gets.

Well, all the work was worth it. A week later, I swept every category in the 1996 international whistling competition. It was a particularly sweet victory that made me feel great, even like a king.

A *Whistle* That Touches My Heart

Name: Thomas B. Heath
Home: Charleston, SC
Job: Life coach, playwright
Thomas' *Whistle*: Boundaries
How I Know Thomas: As first cousins (our mothers are sisters), we've known each other our entire lives.

***Whistle* in Action**: In the poem "Mending Wall," Robert Frost mused about the value of walls separating land and people. Regardless of inefficacy or necessity, Frost lamented, the fellow farmer stuck to his belief that "Good fences make good neighbors." To me, walls—real or metaphorical—are all about respect, so I tend to agree with Frost's neighbor. Over the past ten years in particular, cousin Thomas has helped me realize the power of well-defined and articulated boundaries when it comes to both personal and professional relationships. Boundaries aren't about keeping people out, Thomas reminds me, they're about letting them into our lives in constructive and respectful ways. Here's his personal definition: "Boundaries are an indicator of what is, and what is not, acceptable to me in my life." Thomas is a passionate, creative person, committed to lifelong learning and personal growth. Following years of work and reflection, he has harnessed the power of boundaries to foster peaceful, healthy, and productive environments and relationships. Our close friendship has enabled me to witness the fruits of his journey and importantly, to benefit from them. In keeping with his philosophy, when asked, Thomas readily gives candid, constructive suggestions (he says with a smile that he's very careful about giving "advice"). Many times, he's helped me think through sticky personal and professional situations in ways that are logical and respectful, and when necessary, apply a dose of tough love. I am a healthier, happier person as a result.

CHAPTER 24

Aunt Irene: Rest in Peace

I HAD PERFORMED AT MANY WEDDINGS, but this was my first funeral. I was very excited, in an appropriate way, curious to see how the whistle worked in a somber setting.

In 2003, my mother-in-law Carole asked me to whistle at her Aunt Irene's graveside service. Carole picked "On Eagle's Wings," a popular funeral song (among the living, that is). There's never a dry eye in the house (of worship) with that song. I hoped I'd be able to make it through without tearing up. Though I've never whistled while weepy, I don't think they'd go together well.

With four verses and a refrain, the song can go on for a good three minutes. The words are comforting, ethereal: "You who dwell in the shelter of the Lord / Who abide in His shadow for life / Say to the Lord / 'My refuge, my rock in whom I trust!'" The refrain is exquisite: "And He will raise you up on eagle's wings / Bear you on the breath of dawn / Make you to shine like the sun / And hold you in the palm of His hand."

It was a drizzly day. Twenty or so family and friends were gathered beside the gravesite under a tent, some sitting and some standing. The casket rested upon a metal support above the six-foot hole. Green Astroturf shielded sad hearts from the dirt. At the appointed time, I stepped forward and started whistling, the song book in my hands as the words of comfort coursed through my brain.

One verse in, things were going well. I had the eagle-wing mojo going. Then I segued into the refrain, the part that gets most people. The image of being raised up by a loving God while nestled in his hand is great stuff. The composer, Michael Joncas, captured so well what so many of us hope for. It's practical and poetic.

After the refrain, I launched into the second verse. I was fully en-meshed in the song, my eyes closed and my body gently swaying. As I transitioned from the second verse back into the refrain, I opened my eyes. Carole, whose back had been toward me, half-turned and made the 'hand slashing across the throat' gesture...all with a smile, of course. Other than me, I think only my wife noticed.

I wasn't sure what the problem was, but it seemed prudent to keep Carole happy. So, with a slight ritard, I brought the eagle in for a landing.

At the reception afterwards, my wife explained her mom's con-cern. It was a quantity problem, not a quality issue. While I'd had the words traversing through my brain, the mourners only heard the same melody and refrain over and over. So, after two verses of word-free whistling, Carole was satisfied that the eagle had soared high enough.

CHAPTER 25
Life Lessons Lip-Learned

THE GENIUS ARTIST–SCULPTOR MICHELANGELO, when asked about one of his greatest works, said he didn't create, he revealed. Within the twenty-foot tall block of marble that other sculptors had rejected, Michelangelo envisioned David, the giant slayer. It was Michelangelo's job to set the stone-clad captive free.

Several years ago for my fiftieth birthday, my wife and I visited with David at the Accademia Gallery in Florence, Italy. After spending more than an hour circling him, necks craned, examining every nook and cranny, I concluded that Michelangelo was being a bit too humble. But then, who am I to question the creative genius of the greatest artist in human history? Whether he was created or revealed, all I know is that David exists and he is stunning.

Taking a cue from the great sculptor, as we travel on this journey called life, we should ask ourselves a question: are we creating or revealing? When it comes to who we are as individuals, I'd say it's mostly a process of creation. We are for the most part blank slates, our genetics notwithstanding. Day in and day out, year after year, we construct ourselves, piece by piece, brick by brick, absorbing information, growing, stumbling, achieving, and hopefully, developing wisdom. The physical and mental development of a human across the years of his or her life is miraculous, the greatest act of creation the world has known.

On the other hand, when it comes to understanding the world, and how to succeed and be happy within it, I believe it's all about revelation. Scripture sums it up well. Ecclesiastes 1:9 says: "What has been will be again, what has been done will be done again; there is nothing new under the sun." Simply put, all the building blocks of everyday life already exist. They may be out of focus, jumbled, and obscured, but they are there—always have been, always will be.

For example, we don't create Newton's laws of physics; rather, we learn how to fall down-go boom as toddlers and weather the ravages of gravity as we age. It's the same with human nature. You and I didn't create the seven deadly sins; they've existed since the beginning of humanity, and don't seem to be dying out. As we grow and mature, though, it's in our best interest to reveal, understand, and manage them.

So, unlike our individual development, the process of learning about the world, and how to function within it, is akin to that giant block of marble. Like Michelangelo, chisel at the ready, our job is to reveal things, facts and truths, then to experience and grow as we try to make sense of it all.

We all have our means of discovery. A particularly effective tool for me has been my lips. Whistling has helped me reveal how life works, what is important, and how to make the most of every day. That has helped to make me happy. That doesn't mean you have to whistle to be happy, though it certainly helps.

What have my lips helped reveal in nearly fifty years of whistling? Here are the four core lessons:

1. Be humble
2. Be grateful
3. Be open-minded
4. Be disciplined

The pursuit of excellence, whether you are a whistler, an investment banker, a car mechanic, or a nurse, sets the stage to learn these things and many others. That doesn't mean I have perfected them—I haven't. It's a journey, and I'm around two-thirds of the way there.

Be Humble – Life Is Difficult, Now Get on With It

"David, I wanted to let you know that I have a whistling CD coming out, and that I may be getting some media attention. Please know that I'm committed to Carlyle."

"I'm not worried," he said with a wry smile. "We pay you more than you'll ever make whistling."

With that candid assessment, my boss reminded me that however grand my whistling dreams, it's not a profession that could ever sustain me financially—at least not at a Carlyle-level of income.

Ouch! Any reasonable person would agree with David, but I, as well as several other accomplished whistlers, hoped that turning our avocation into a financially lucrative vocation was only one good news article, championship trophy, or TV appearance away from reality. But life rarely works that way.

For whistlers, take-downs and put downs are par for the course. Take the newbie whistling competitors. They are the sole whistlers in their home, family, school, club, or community. No one within earshot whistles as well, or at least as frequently and loudly. For years, they have regaled people at parties or through snippets heard while walking the dog.

"Beautiful." "Amazing." "How do you do that?" "I can't even whistle…you're great." The accumulated accolades are heartfelt and subjectively accurate. Like the person on that fateful 1992 hike in the Shenandoah who told me I should do something with my whistling, many of the contestants at the international competition have heard the same thing time and again.

As we all know, dreams colliding with reality can be quite messy. Over the years, I've seen many whistlers at the international competition get blown out of the water, not even advancing to the final round, let alone winning any prizes. That's a tough pill to swallow when you've been told how talented you are all your life.

The range of reaction is wide. Most suck it up and vow to do better next time, while a few are shocked and cry foul. From the complainers, the organizers of the competition have heard it all: "The judges are biased…the rules aren't clear or fair…the machine playing the backup music is defective." In eleven years of competing in and judging the competition, I never experienced or witnessed any bias. That doesn't mean everything and everyone was perfect. Nothing ever is. Best I can tell, though, the organizers and judges worked hard to be fair to all competitors, and they did it all for free. None of them ever took a salary, and among the organizers, none of them was even a whistler.

I understand why people are upset when they lose. Ego is powerful. It's a great motivator. Would we have iPhones if Steve Jobs was not madly driven to achieve? We can go through life thinking the world owes us something, or we can focus on earned success. The latter, I believe, is so much more satisfying. It requires, when things don't go as planned or hoped, that we look first in the mirror to see what we did wrong or could have done better. Only after that should we look elsewhere for causes to our disappointment. But who wants to be that blunt with themselves? It's hard and can be pretty ugly.

Competitions that rely on subjective scoring (versus the time-clock), will always be tougher on the ego. Though I won the grand championship four out of nine times, that means I lost five times—four of which were not pleasant. (I had zero expectations the first time I competed, so coming in second in the 'popular' division was a great and unexpected treat.)

Two of the nine times I competed, I thought I was a shoe-in for grand champion, but came in second one time and won nothing another year. The time I walked away with nothing (the 1997 international competition), I was particularly galled. In 1996, I had won every major prize: First Place Popular; First Place Classical, and First Place Grand Champion. That year, I was also given the Lillian Williams Whistler of the Year award. As I had looked to defend my crown, I had momentum, mojo, and confidence in large quantities. I prepared vigorously and gave it my best. Despite all that, I won nothing…NOTHING! I was shocked and disappointed.

It was especially tough to go home and have to confront my family, friends, and media, who assumed I would win again. That humbling experience taught me how to be honest and straightforward. When people asked how I did, I didn't beat around the bush. I actually found that speaking of the smack-down with explicit and even colorful language helped me accept it.

I got used to saying, "I got blown out of the water. The guy who won, Tanguay Desgagne, a fantastic whistler from Canada, did a great job and deserved it." I approached my loss in 2004 the same way. That was supposed to be my comeback after a three-year break, but I tied for third place in the grand championship. To keep myself honest through the years, I've always said I tied for third, rather than just cutting corners and saying I came in third place. It is accurate, fair to the guy I tied with, and I find it liberating to be so precisely honest about an unpleasant thing.

After the 1997 blow-out, I licked my wounds, redoubled my efforts, and two years later, I won the first of back-to-back championships. Following a three-year drought, those final victories were particularly satisfying.

Among many other humbling whistling experiences, one stands out. In 2003, I convinced my wife that we should spend $30,000 to produce a whistling CD. I wanted to get it right the first time, so I hired a project manager, an assistant, a forty-two piece symphony orchestra, an experienced conductor, and a CD fabrication house. A year later, the CD was done, and it was time to sell them. It was a fascinating experience that taught me a lot about myself and human nature in general.

Unexpectedly, strangers and acquaintances excitedly bought CDs by the dozen (one guy bought fifty...everyone on his Christmas list got one). This heartened me. Meanwhile, some close friends and family members took a pass and didn't even buy one. One person even came to my CD launch party and left without one. In the scheme of things, it was an inconsequential outcome, but it was among the most humbling experiences of my whistling career.

This is when a loving and clear-eyed spouse especially comes in handy. My pouting was met with tough love. Kristen reminded me of my Libertarian views: people should be free to do what they want. She asked if I wanted my friends to buy CDs because they felt obligated to do so, or worse, because they felt sorry for me. Of course not, I said. But it still hurt. I developed a new appreciation for an expression I had employed for years: Life is difficult, now get on with it.

On the other end of the spectrum, whistling also taught me how to humbly and confidently accept compliments. That may seem like a contradiction, but it's not—they are opposite sides of the same coin. Responding to well wishes from someone can be tricky. You don't want to be too cocky and act like your award-winning performance was easy, like you could have knocked it off in your sleep. Nor do you want to wrap yourself in faux humility and say you're shocked you won, or point out all the mistakes the person offering the compliments obviously missed.

What I learned over time is to respect the judgment of the person saying nice things, whether he or she is a music critic or the owner of a tin ear. If someone says, "I really enjoyed your performance," there's only one proper response: "You are kind to say that...thanks very much." Full stop. No explaining or qualifying, otherwise you risk insulting the person offering the compliment.

Just last night, I whistled "Happy Birthday" at a friend's fiftieth birthday party. Afterwards, a number of people came up to me and said nice things and asked how I developed this talent. If it's the first or the thousandth time, the response has to be the same: "Thank you very much."

Be Grateful – Every Day Is a Gift

In my early teens, filled with typical life-angst (*Who am I and what is all this stuff about?*), I came upon a poem in an Ann Landers advice column titled "The Station," by Robert Hastings. It offered a simple but powerful way of thinking and living that immediately appealed to me.

For the past forty years, I have tried to live by the maxim captured in the poem: happiness is a manner of traveling, not a destination. Every day is a gift, it said. Climb more mountains, eat more ice cream, laugh more, cry less, because "one of these days, may be none of these days."

One might think this is a license for short-term thinking and behavior, but that misses the point. Life is a continuum. Today is what you've got, but it is the entrée to tomorrow's similarly unique day. They are separate and linked at the same time. Making the most of today need not come at the expense of tomorrow. Prudence coupled with a sense of adventure is the balance I've struck.

I realized early on, while delivering newspapers as a thirteen year-old, that whistling is a tool that helps me make the most of every day. Back then, it was primarily about making beautiful music happen rather than just thinking about it. Riding along on my Schwinn Stingray while whistling great classical pieces was an amazing experience. It was me and my lips communing with Beethoven or Mozart or Brahms. It helped make a mundane task enjoyable, and my days sweeter. I will always be grateful for that.

As I got older and better, though, I saw how I could use my simple gift to touch people's hearts and lives through performance, competition, birthday serenades, and storytelling. To me, two of the most important things in life are people and experiences. Whistling has given me gobs of exposure to both. For that, I am also immensely grateful. Actually, I'm shocked and grateful. As I survey all the things I've done with my whistling, I'm amazed at how blessed I've been. I never could have imagined meeting the people I have or doing the things I've been able to do. Simply put, whistling has changed the course of my life.

When I was in the Oval Office whistling for President Bush, I said to myself several times, *Remember every moment of this, because it's the coolest and freakiest thing you will ever do…and it will never happen again.* The same feeling consumed me when I was 555 feet in the air, perched atop the Washington Monument, whistling "Yankee Doodle" in honor of our first president, and when I stood before China's top banker, as my whistling launched him into an idyllic state. Even when people tell me I made their day with a birthday whistle, it's a magical feeling to touch a heart with my lips. (It's not as messy as it sounds!)

In trying to live the message of "The Station," making the most of every day, I've developed a talent that first brought me great joy, then over time turned into a means to touch other people's lives in simple ways, bringing delight and wonder to them. Their affirming reactions reinforce my behavior. It's an awesome positive feedback loop. (That said, I still whistle for myself when I'm alone because it makes me happy; I'm just incredibly delighted that I can share it with other people.)

I often tell my kids that every day is a gift. At first, they had no idea what I meant. Now my regular admonishments are met with grunts and some eye-rolling. Someday, though, I hope they will embrace this simple truth: today is unique, and will never happen again—be grateful for it and make the most of it.

Be Open-Minded – Try It, You'll Be Better for It

Washington, DC, my home of thirty years, is riddled with sycophants, suck-ups who tell the boss what he or she wants to hear. I'm so concerned about the practice that when I interview someone for a job on my team, I ask him or her about their ability to speak truth to power. I'm interested in people who are good at telling the boss what they *need* to hear, not what they *want* to hear. Such people are hard to find.

Receiving constructive criticism, whether you're a politician, businessperson, or whistler, is the key to becoming the best you can be.

When the boss gives license to subordinates to critique his or her work and the person has the courage to deliver thoughtful and focused suggestions for improvement, it's a beautiful thing. The mission trumps ego. It's not about knocking someone down, but moving toward the goal.

I give the same advice to college seniors whom I mentor. If you want real feedback about your strengths and weaknesses, don't ask your parents. They are rarely capable of being brutally honest. Instead, find people who care about you and have some measure of objectivity, then give them license to constructively criticize. When I want unconditional love and a sweet "atta-boy," I go to my mom, Fran Ullman. When I seek tough love in the whistling department, I go elsewhere. My mom is not capable of giving constructive criticism; she's just not wired that way. And that's okay. The key is to be honest with yourself about what you're getting from different people.

I credit Betty Buchanan, my long-time choir conductor, with teaching me to turn notes into music. For ten years, Betty was gently blunt in her musical direction. She taught me what great music was, and for nearly thirty years since first singing in her choir, I have worked to achieve in my whistling what she taught us for voice. (Over the years, I've observed that many of the best whistlers are also accomplished singers…they are remarkably similar instruments.) As a result, I am my own harshest critic, rehearsing my pieces over and over until my lips quiver, and trying new techniques until they are just right. I then try out my pieces on people I know are able and willing to give meaningful feedback. Trying to be the best is a daunting goal that requires constant refinement and improvement.

Betty's great direction helped me solve a persistent problem I had when whistling a cappella. Since I don't have perfect pitch (the ability to sing or whistle a certain note in a certain key without a reference point, such as a piano or pitch pipe), I would sometimes change keys in the middle of a song, especially when jumping up or down the scale. Through Betty, I learned how to notice and correct. Once I started paying attention, my a cappella whistling improved dramatically.

Since much of my whistling (including my annual 400 birthday serenades) is solo, key and pitch are critical.

I've long been fascinated by people who are wholly uninterested in receiving criticism, constructive or otherwise. They never ask for help, and give you the evil eye or a sharp retort when unsolicited advice comes their way. It's sad when people's fragile egos stand in the way of achieving all they are capable of. These folks aren't necessarily doomed, but their journeys are more difficult than they need to be.

There is a different way. Over the years, I've had clients who, within moments of giving a speech or a media interview, ask for feedback, particularly constructive criticism. They are confident yet humble, knowing that everyone can eke out some improvement with a little effort. These are my favorite clients, because helping people grow is challenging and satisfying.

Since no one I know actually likes to be criticized, it does take time and practice to get good at receiving meaningful feedback. For me, there are two main parts: the giver must be able and willing to criticize, and the recipient must be open to receiving it. To fulfill my end of the bargain, I develop goals that I know I can't achieve without help; then I find people who have my best interests at heart and are competent and honest. It's magical when both pieces click together. By letting down my defenses and welcoming thoughtful feedback, I've achieved far more than I ever imagined possible.

Be Disciplined – Liberating by Confining

"Daddy, I want an Oompa Loompa! I want you to get me an Oompa Loompa right away! I want an Oompa Loompa now."

This is my favorite line from the original movie version of *Willie Wonka and the Chocolate Factory*. The spoiled and impetuous Veruca Salt has just met an Oompa Loompa, a living, breathing human-like being, and tells her father that she must have one...now! He promises to get her one right away.

Veruca lacks discipline. It's all about the here and now. Instant desires must be instantly filled. Conversely, discipline is all about delaying today's wants for tomorrow's needs.

Discipline is probably the most important tool needed to achieve one's goals. Simply put, discipline liberates by confining; if you do this *one* thing today, you can do these *two* things tomorrow.

Discipline is a learned trait. Step by step, it must be grown and nurtured, pruned and refined. Learning to be disciplined has been a great journey in my whistling career. When I was most disciplined, I won; when I slacked off, resting on my laurels, I lost.

Discipline manifests itself in many ways, but practice is the most obvious. People often ask me if I have to practice. It used to startle me, but now I understand why people ask, and I respond straight-away, "Of course…at least two hours a day when preparing for a performance or competition." Same as with a violinist, opera singer, or cyclist, practice is the best expression of love for one's vocation. (That people ask the question is another indication that whistlers have much work to do to demonstrate that our lips are actual instruments and whistling is art.)

The beauty of whistling is that it is lightweight and portable. Have lips and air, will practice—driving in the car, walking down the street, in the parking garage, at home beside the piano, sequestered in the basement away from beleaguered spouses and sleeping children, you name it. I dedicate hundreds of hours to mastering my pieces. I break them down part by part, first to get the notes, then to arrange the piece for whistle. Using different techniques and sounds, I try to breathe life into the pieces in a way that reflects my personality.

Why am I disciplined? Over the years, I've learned that if you have big dreams, you need to be incredibly disciplined to achieve them. For me, discipline is the fruit of a positive feedback loop. Discipline begets achievement, which begets pleasure, which encourages more discipline, because pleasure (winning and accolades) is desirable.

Less-disciplined people are stuck in a negative feedback loop. Short-term thinking yields problems, which require solving, which distract from their long-term goals, which set them back even further financially and emotionally, which yields more pleasure-centric short-term behavior, and so on.

These are obvious simplifications of complex behaviors, as everyone's situation is unique. Depending on where you are on the discipline spectrum will determine how much effort it will take to become more disciplined. For folks looking to make progress in this area, I'm a big fan of baby steps. In my day job, one of my management philosophies is to 'embrace incrementalism'. While bold strokes can be effective at work and in life, small, consistent steps are more likely to bring about change and get you to your goal. (This approach is similar to the juxtaposition of heroic behavior versus the development of simple gifts that this book is about.)

Also, finding people (or dogs) who inspire you can be helpful on the journey of improved discipline. For example, I've long been motivated by champion cyclists, since I am an avid road biker. Professional cycling is arguably the most demanding sport in the world. Look at the Tour de France: 2,200 miles in three weeks, at speeds averaging twenty-five to twenty-eight miles per hour. Incomprehensible—if you're not into biking, trust me, this is astounding. But they are able to do it because of the discipline of training, illegal doping notwithstanding. To come close to the Yellow Jersey, they train like fiends—fifty to 100-mile rides at incredible speeds, six days a week, for months on end, year after year.

Such commitment to excellence and achievement boggles my mind and spurs me on to do my best, to find patterns and rhythms that will enable me to grow as a musician, and to fine-tune my art in ways that differentiate me in competitions and delight audiences at performances.

Another example of discipline that has intrigued me for nearly thirty years is the steely discipline of a friend's dog. My dear friend Pete Brown used to have a dog named Breef (Pete is a lawyer). Pete trained Breef to accept a biscuit in his mouth, but not chew it until allowed to do so. I saw it with my own eyes and was amazed. Breef is long gone, but his example of remarkable discipline lives on. Over the years I often thought, *If Breef can do it, so can I.*

Sometimes people ask me *how* disciplined I am. On a scale of one to ten, I give myself a seven and a half. This is an improvement from my high school days, but compared to some hyper-disciplined friends, I still have a ways to go. One buddy is a serious swimmer. He's up at 4:14 every morning to get to the pool in time for his workout, to ensure he can be in the office by 7:30. We talked recently, and he was on his thirtieth straight day of this intense routine—impressive. And that discipline has helped him become a successful businessman, husband and father. It permeates every aspect of his life and enables him to do his best and gets him closer to his full potential.

I also do a crazy thing that helps me develop and strengthen my discipline. I'm a dessert lover who gives up all dessert every other year...for the full year. Yes, *all* dessert: cakes, cookies, ice cream, candy bars, you name it. I started this in 1999, and have found the bi-annual fast to be an amazing tool for improving my overall discipline. Discipline, I've found, is a state of being that applies to a range of circumstances—when I wake up, what I eat, how often I practice whistling, my exercise regime, frequency of prayer, and a hundred other things.

You may be wondering how this meshes with my goal to make the most of every day, which calls for eating more ice cream, among other delightful things. It's all about balance and trade-offs. In general, I eat too much dessert, so this is a radical way to help regulate my consumption. Of course, moderation would be best, and I'm working on that. In the meantime, though, I find that the sweet-free fast makes me more disciplined overall and, importantly, helps me to embrace the concept of delayed gratification, which, I believe, was critical to my whistling success in particular and my long-term happiness in general.

Don't believe me? Just ask Veruca Salt.

———————

"It is well with me only when I have a chisel in my hand."
Michelangelo

As the great Michelangelo chiseled away at the marble that contained David, I imagine a hard-to-contain eagerness. With each hammer strike, David came closer to the surface; then appeared a languid curl, the angle of his cheekbone, determined eyes. It must have been more of a reunion than a first-time meeting.

As we work to create ourselves and reveal the ways of the world, striving for understanding, happiness, and impact, let us, like the master, imbued with urgency, *find our whistles* and get to work.

CHAPTER 26

Happy Birthday, Happy Whistler

I PRESSED THE PLAY BUTTON on my iPhone voicemail and out came a joyful noise. A friend was puckering and blowing for my birthday. About halfway through, the creaky sound was supplanted by giggling, and then followed by renewed efforts to finish what the friend had started. I smiled broadly.

It warms my heart when people whistle for me. I don't care about the quality; it's the effort that counts.

Over the years, I've found that it takes a lot of courage for someone to whistle for me, whether on a phone message or in person. I occasionally meet people who say that they love to whistle. The reaction when I ask him or her to whistle is always the same: "Well, compared to you, I'm not that good." My perennial response is: "I promote whistling at all levels. No need to compare. The goal is to get more people whistling." With that invitation, I can usually get them to produce a few notes.

If people want feedback, I'm happy to give it. If they simply want to share their literal whistle, that's okay too. I've met some pretty good whistlers over the years, who, with some training and serious initiative, could go places with their whistle. And I've met many people who say they can't whistle at all, which they are usually eager to prove. In these cases, the absence of ability affords absolution, while having limited ability is perceived as a handicap, even embarrassing.

A few times over the years, I've had roomfuls of people whistle "Happy Birthday" for me. As I scan the gathering of puckerers, a kaleidoscope of images and sounds mingle and jell into simple sweetness. I see giggly people struggling to form a pucker, while some belt out the birthday tune and others resort to humming. There's a joy and frivolity that embraces the group the way a simply sung "Happy Birthday" never could. I close my eyes and revel in the sound. I feel loved. Though I never expect people to reciprocate with a whistle on my birthday, it does warm my heart to have friends whose efforts express a simple, caring message.

CHAPTER 27
Brendan Kelly: A Life That Touched Many Hearts

THE E-MAIL STARTED OUT as many do: a request to support a worthy cause, in this case the Leukemia & Lymphoma Society annual fundraiser in Washington, DC.

It was the second sentence that nearly knocked me off my chair: "As you know, our precious son Brendan passed away in May 2013."

Stunned and filled with dread, embarrassment and guilt welled up in my throat. Somehow I didn't know that Brendan had died, and therefore had continued to whistle "Happy Birthday" to him for three years after he passed. The first time was only two weeks after his lengthy battle with leukemia took him to the Lord.

Like it was yesterday, I remember when I learned that Brendan was ill. His father Frank and I ran into each other at New York's LaGuardia Airport shuttle lounge in 2009. Though only casual acquaintances, Frank and I are always delighted to see each other. He lives in the Washington, DC area and travels to New York often, as do I, so such meetings on the shuttle are common.

Not only did Brendan have leukemia, but he was also born with Down Syndrome, a genetic disorder that causes a range of physical and cognitive challenges. Frank told me of his then nine year-old son with a combination of pride and resolve. They were working hard to beat the illness that had invaded his little body. As the father of three young healthy children, I had no idea of what his life was like on a daily basis, but I imagined it was hard.

I said that the Ullmans would pray for Brendan, and I asked when his birthday was, so I could whistle for him. There wasn't much else I could do.

So the Ullmans set to praying for little Brendan. We have a daily prayer list that includes people who are sick, those who need jobs, and people who would like to be married and have babies ("Preferably in that order," I sometimes add, to my young children's confusion).

In a twist, there were two other people on our prayer list who had Brendan's last name, "Kelly," in their names. There was Kelly Martin, Cara Kelly, and now we added Brendan Kelly. Kelly and Cara both had cancer.

Our kids had never met any of them, but embraced praying for them as if they were family. Our son Justus, who was six years old when we started praying for Brendan, would sometimes ask who these people were. Kelly was a friend of Mommy's from Bible study, Cara was the daughter of Uncle Dale's friend, and Brendan was the son of a friend of Daddy's.

The prayers continued for years, seeking healing, but praying that "Thy will be done."

Several years in, we learned that Cara beat her cancer. Then Kelly succumbed to her illness, and Brendan went into remission. When Kelly died, the kids asked what happened. We said that she fought hard and the doctors did their best, but the Lord called her to his heavenly kingdom. "Did our prayers not work?" the kids asked. I wondered the same thing, but reminded myself that discerning God's will is a fool's errand. We talk of His omnipotence and omniscience, but have little understanding of what that means. All knowing, all powerful—His ways are not our ways. We seek mercy and healing, and sometimes it comes, sometimes not—at least not always in the form we would like. We forge on, hopefully appreciating the great gift of life while it is ours and accepting His will, with its mysteries and sometimes seeming illogic.

As I recovered from my initial shock of having whistled "Happy Birthday" for someone who was no longer alive, I quickly wrote an e-mail to Frank, apologizing for adding to his heartache.

Frank's response floored me.

He said they thought I knew and was honoring Brendan by celebrating his birth and life. The family, he said, would gather around the speakerphone and listen to my recorded rendition as they remembered his birthday. He called it a blessing.

Then he brought a smile to my face. Brendan so enjoyed my annual birthday serenades, he taught himself to whistle. Frank wrote, "What you don't know is that your whistling convinced him to try and learn to whistle. And he did—it wasn't perfect, but it was the most beautiful thing in the world watching my little Down Syndrome guy pucker his beautiful little lips together and whistle a happy song. We knew when he whistled he was happy and being a normal kid, not a sick kid."

Frank ended his note this way: "...please please please: keep leaving the birthday whistle message!"

Imagine that—a father asks me to help keep the spirit of his son alive through a simple song; a son my wife and kids and I never met, but formed a bond with nonetheless, a kid who battled and beat a cruel illness three times until he couldn't fight any more. He was a child of God who was challenged with Down Syndrome, but who touched many lives: 3,000 people attended his wake.

So, what will I do on every May 12 for as long as my lips will cooperate?

Deliver a simple serenade to Frank and his family as they remember and honor their son Brendan.

EPILOGUE

I CAN WHISTLE with my mouth closed. Really.

It's the ultimate stupid human trick.

Some readers will remember how comic David Letterman made the search for stupid human tricks a staple of his late-night TV show. Upon discovering this freaky ability (I hesitate to call it a skill), I dreamt of appearing on *Letterman* to expand people's notions of what the human mouth was capable of. There was one problem: it's very difficult to hear it. When I demonstrate it for people, I have to get my face right next to their ears. Not everyone is comfortable with that, and it would be totally unworkable on TV, its breathtaking stupidity notwithstanding.

I love the reaction from people when I tell them of this unusual trick. Total incredulity meets my claim. "Prove it," they command.

So I sidle up real close and do my thing.

"I hear it! How do you do that?"

First, I say, you need to be able to whistle with your tongue. Then you close your mouth (but don't clench your teeth) and whistle through your tongue in tiny bursts of air. With each gentle blow, cheeks puff up and then deflate instantly to allow for the next note. Muffled, plaintive notes try to break free, but are held captive by closed lips. Open the lips and out flows a song, a whistle touching ears and maybe hearts and lives.

That about sums up what *Find Your Whistle* is all about.

Each one of us is a unique gift from God, with unique skills, desires, opportunities, and challenges. I am a whistler, while Shelby is a journalist and Helen is a politician. It's up to each of us to make the most of our simple gift, to find, develop, and share our *whistles*, not keep them undiscovered or bottled up.

Back when I was five years old and my whistle came to life, I had no idea how powerful it would someday become. The same is true of your *whistle*, dear reader. Within you resides a gift, perhaps several. Have you found it already? Have you tried? Have you touched a heart and changed a life? If not, what's stopping you?

Think of the *whistles* that have impacted your life, warmed your heart, spurred your curiosity, comforted your soul, nourished your brain, and lifted you up. The list of people whose *whistles* have touched my heart is long. I featured a handful of them in this book, but there are many more—my parents, my sister, my best friends Pete Brown, Sofia Hubscher, and Rob Siegel. I am so blessed to have such thoughtful, giving, loving people in my life.

In my day job as a communicator, there's an expression I use to help my clients understand the news business: *Planes that crash make news; planes that land safely don't.* A plane crash garners instant and sustained news coverage. It's a compelling combo of mayhem, gore, and uniqueness…planes just don't crash that often. Meanwhile, every day, tens of thousands of commercial flights take off and land safely, and you never hear a word about it.

Heroism, like plane crashes, is rare—that's why it attracts attention. But it cannot sustain us, as individuals or as a culture. Just as we need planes that land safely (lots of them), we need countless *whistles* making the world a better place.

For nearly fifty years, I've taken the most simple of skills, whistling, something that's been around since the caveman, and used it to touch people's hearts and change lives. It's brought me more joy and satisfaction than I ever imagined possible. It's introduced me to amazing people who've brightened my days and taught me great life lessons. It's enabled me to celebrate life, the greatest gift of all, thousands of times.

I'm not a hero. I'm just a whistler.

What are you?

Have you *found your whistle?*